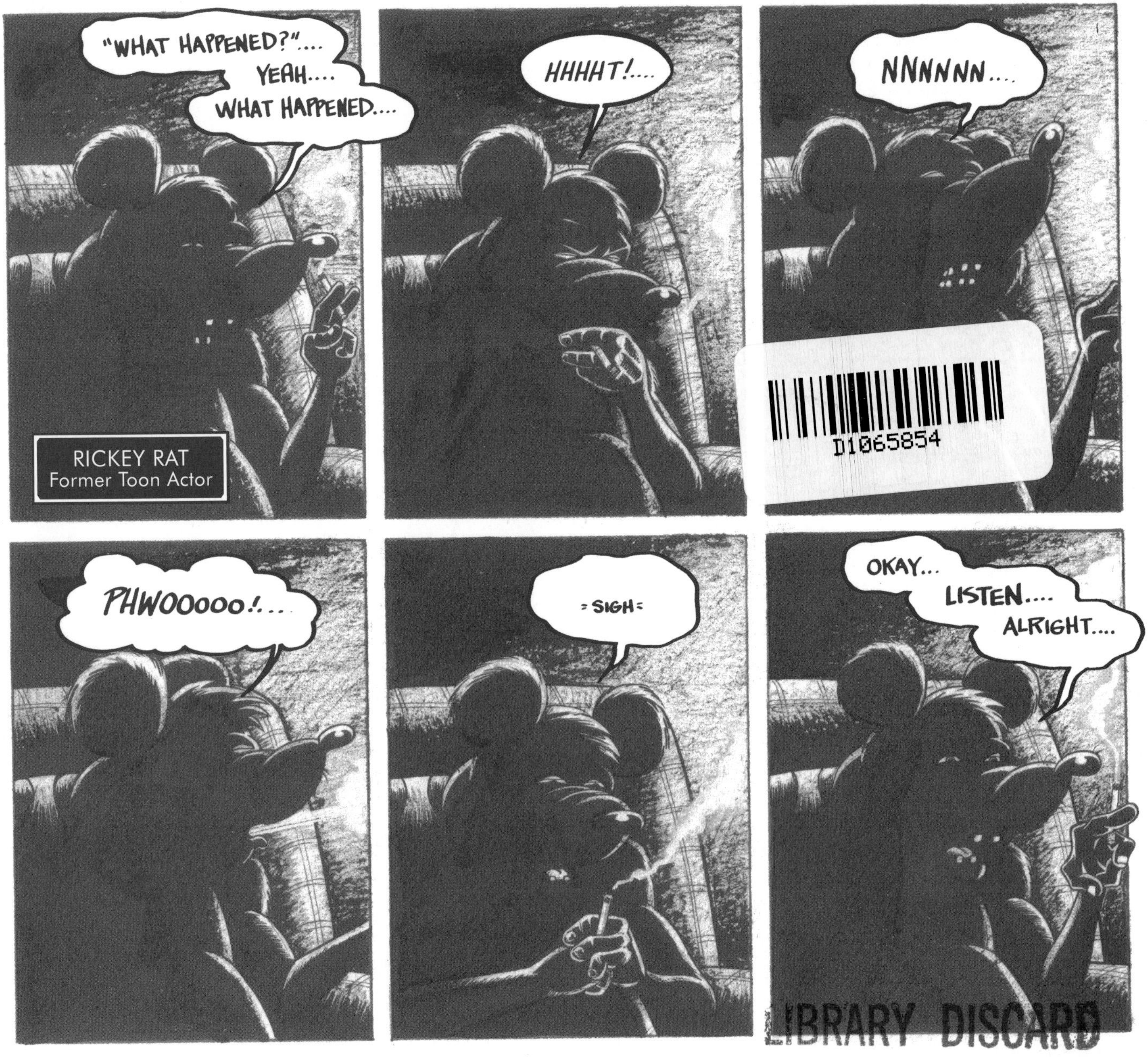
"WHAT HAPPENED?"....
YEAH....
WHAT HAPPENED....
RICKEY RAT
Former Toon Actor
HHHHT!....
NNNNNN....
PHWOOOOO!...
= SIGH =
OKAY...
LISTEN....
ALRIGHT....

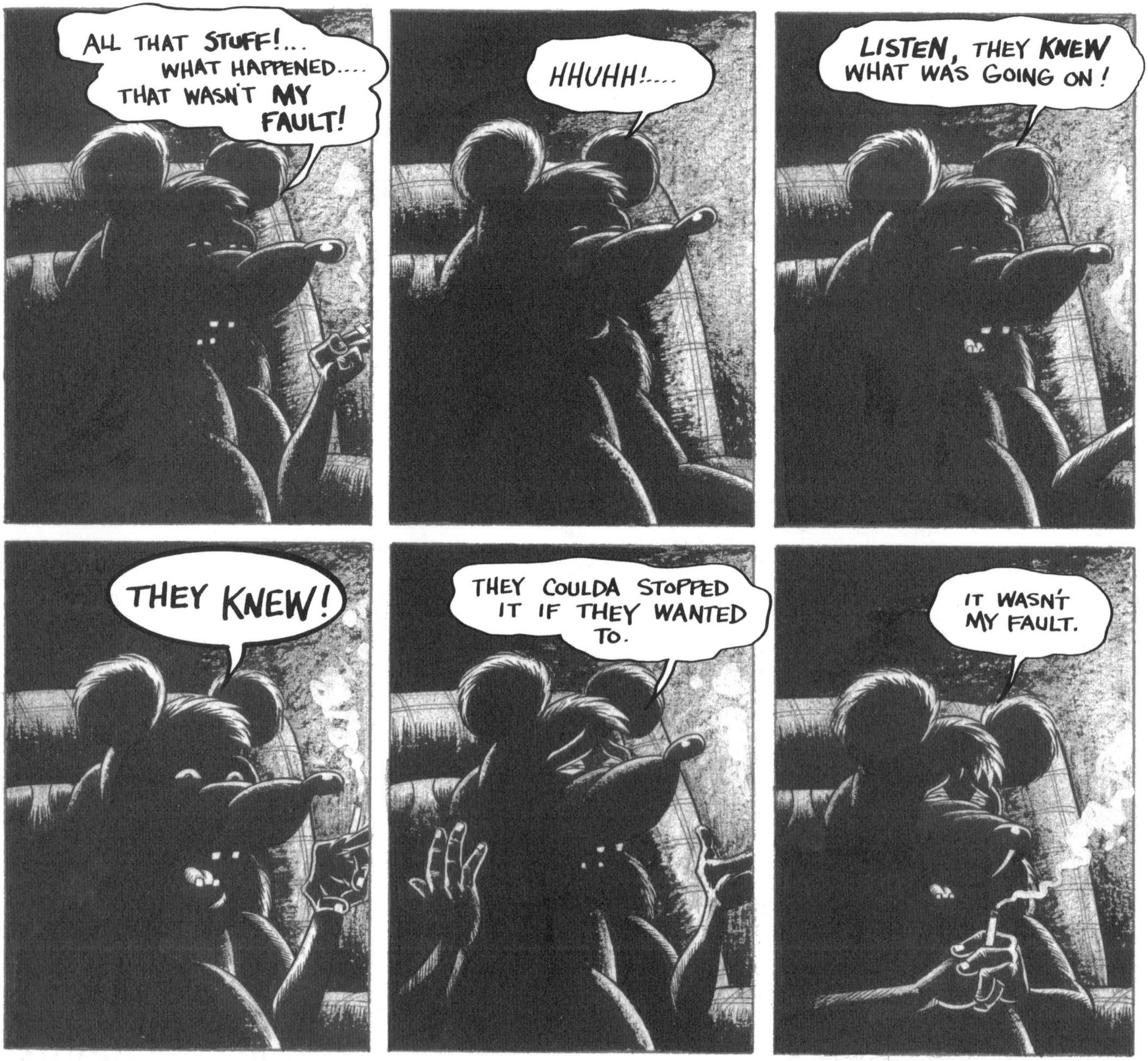
ALL THAT STUFF!... WHAT HAPPENED.... THAT WASN'T MY FAULT!
HHUHH!....
LISTEN, THEY KNEW WHAT WAS GOING ON!
THEY KNEW!
THEY COULDA STOPPED IT IF THEY WANTED TO.
IT WASN'T MY FAULT.

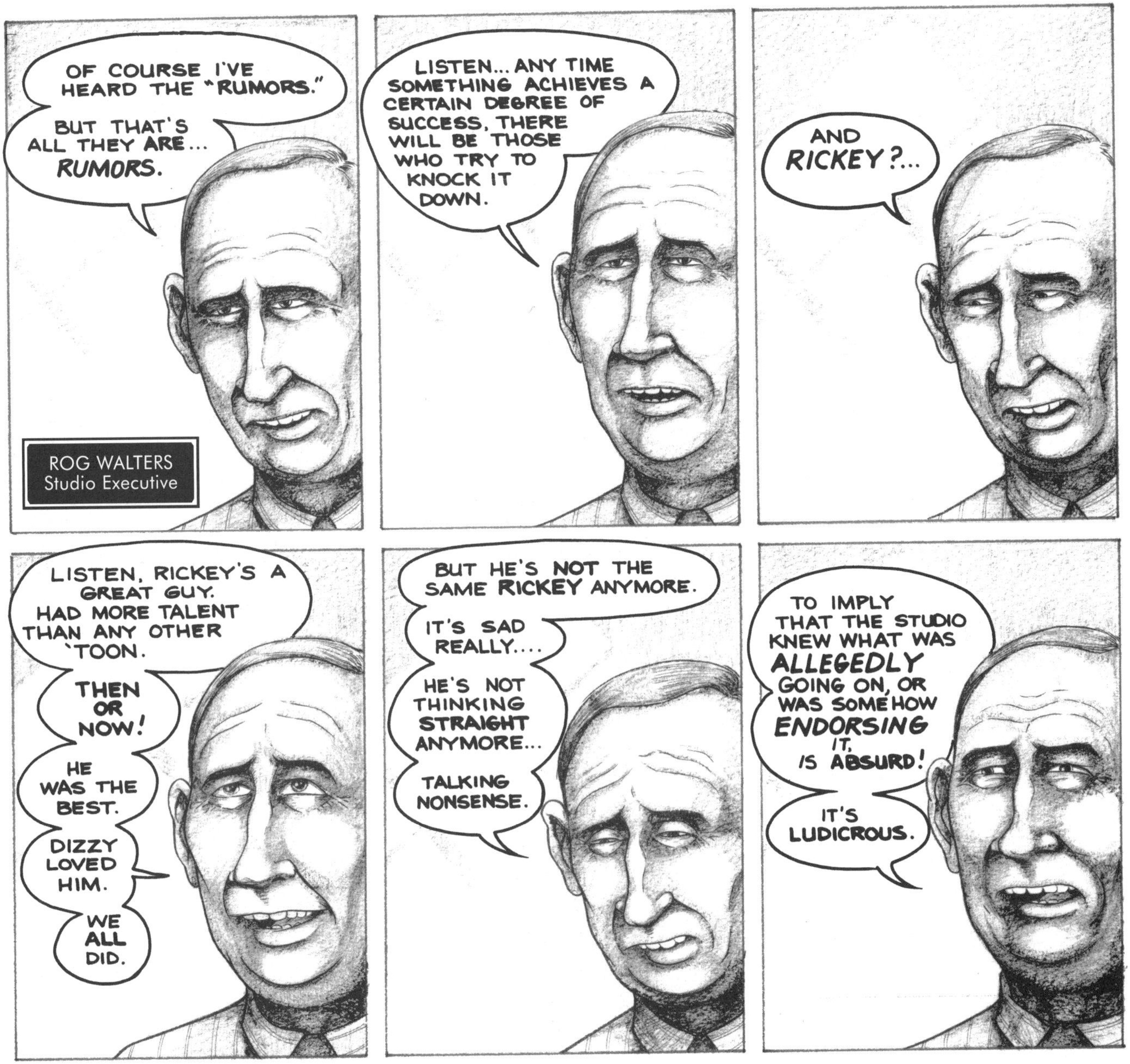
OF COURSE I'VE HEARD THE "RUMORS."
BUT THAT'S ALL THEY ARE... RUMORS.
ROG WALTERS Studio Executive
LISTEN... ANY TIME SOMETHING ACHIEVES A CERTAIN DEGREE OF SUCCESS, THERE WILL BE THOSE WHO TRY TO KNOCK IT DOWN.
AND RICKEY?...
LISTEN, RICKEY'S A GREAT GUY. HAD MORE TALENT THAN ANY OTHER 'TOON.
THEN OR NOW!
HE WAS THE BEST.
DIZZY LOVED HIM.
WE ALL DID.
BUT HE'S NOT THE SAME RICKEY ANYMORE.
IT'S SAD REALLY....
HE'S NOT THINKING STRAIGHT ANYMORE...
TALKING NONSENSE.
TO IMPLY THAT THE STUDIO KNEW WHAT WAS ALLEGEDLY GOING ON, OR WAS SOMEHOW ENDORSING IT, IS ABSURD!
IT'S LUDICROUS.

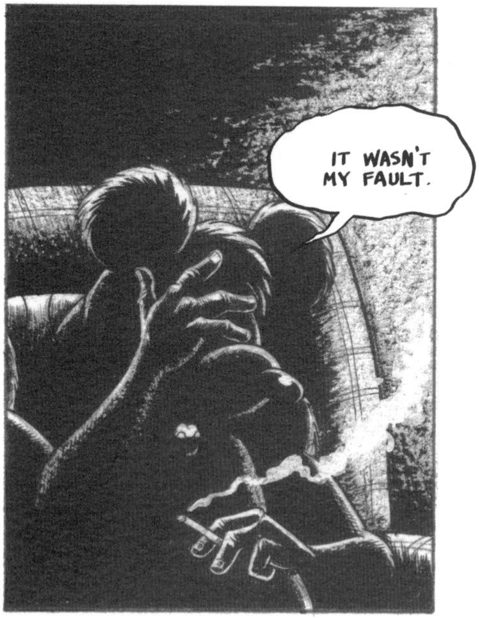
IT WASN'T MY FAULT.

ISBN 978-1-891830-31-0
1. Animation
2. Hollywood "History"
3. Graphic Novels

THREE FINGERS

as told by **rich KOSLOWSKI**

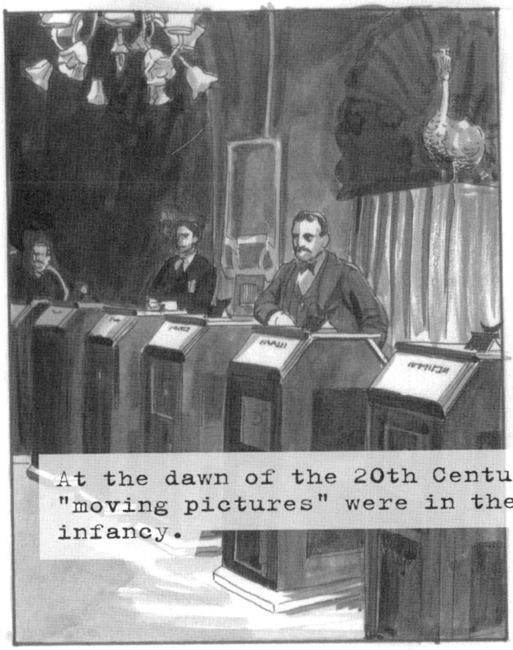
At the dawn of the 20th Century, "moving pictures" were in their infancy.

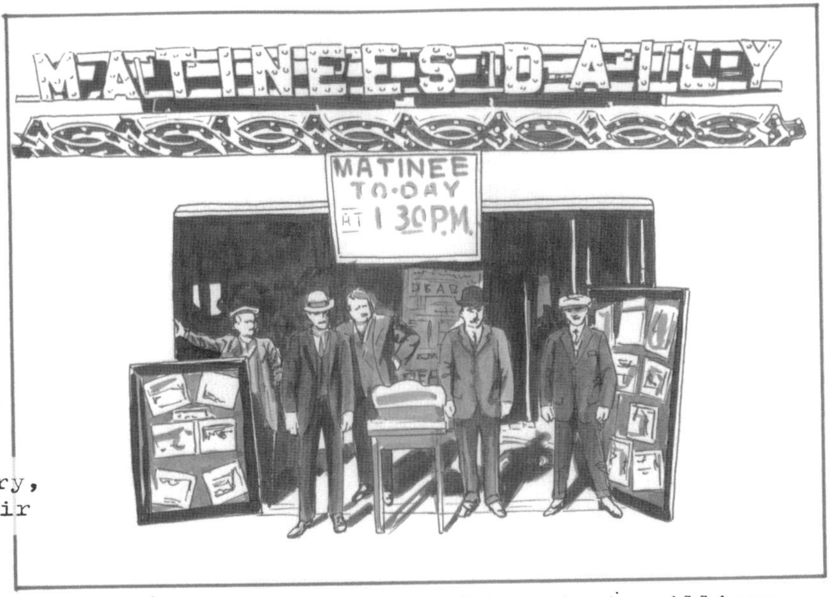
MATINEE
TO-DAY
AT 1 30P.M.

Edison's Kinetoscope brought magic to millions of people across America, in rented barns and small theatres.

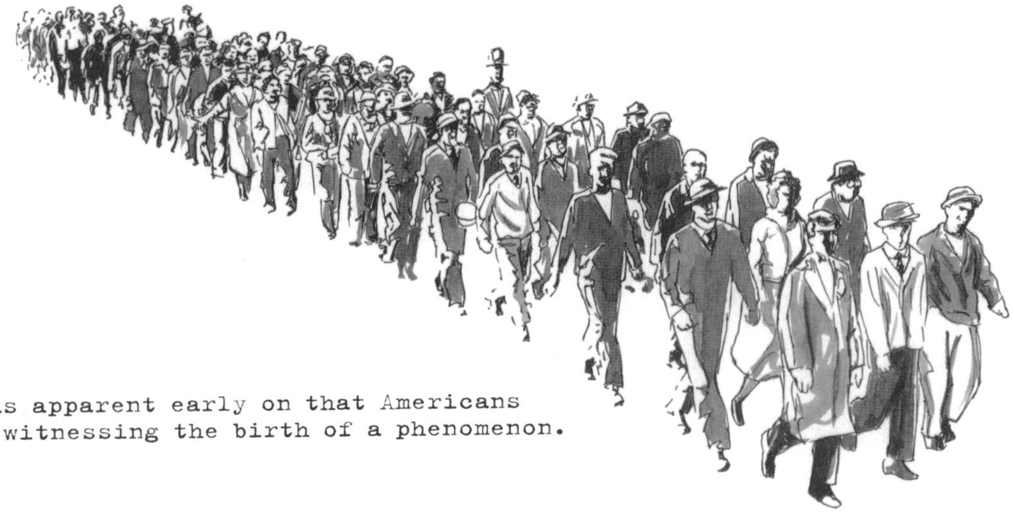

It was apparent early on that Americans were witnessing the birth of a phenomenon.

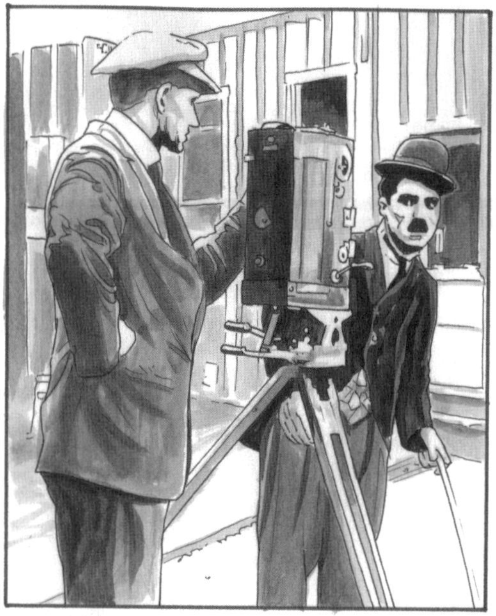

The birth of
a phenomenon...
and the birth of
the first film
superstars.

As the
superstars
emerged,
so did the
"super-
studios."

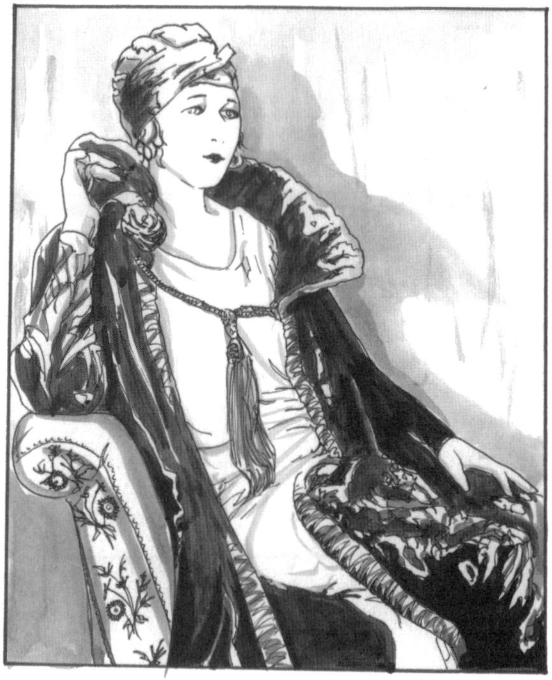

WARMER BROTHERS was one such studio-- Blazing a trail through moving pictures' early years by signing top talent, producing quality films, and daring to take a chance.

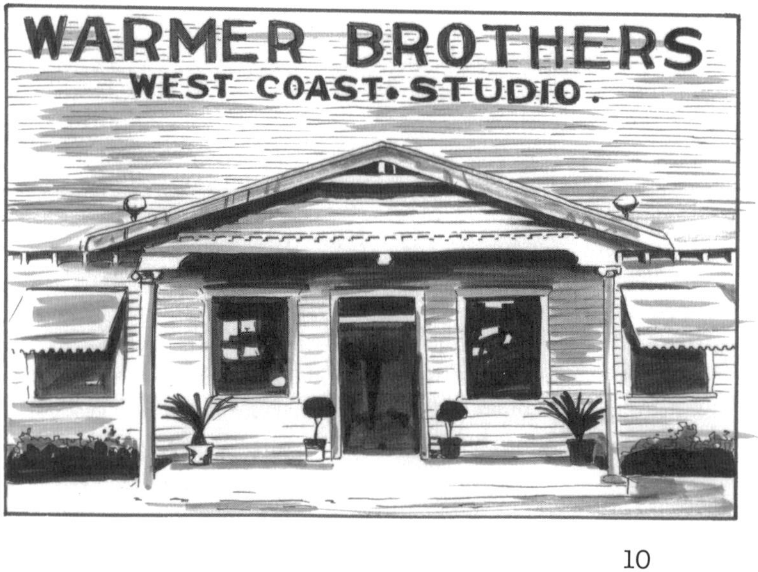
WARMER BROTHERS
WEST COAST. STUDIO.

The "chance" that they dared was dismissed by most other studios initially as being too costly... A passing fad.

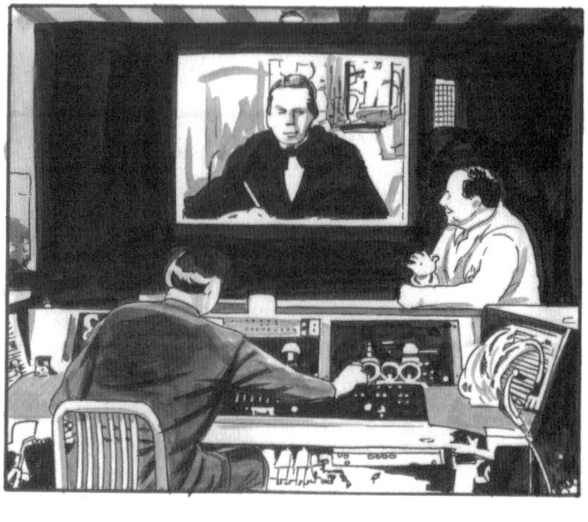

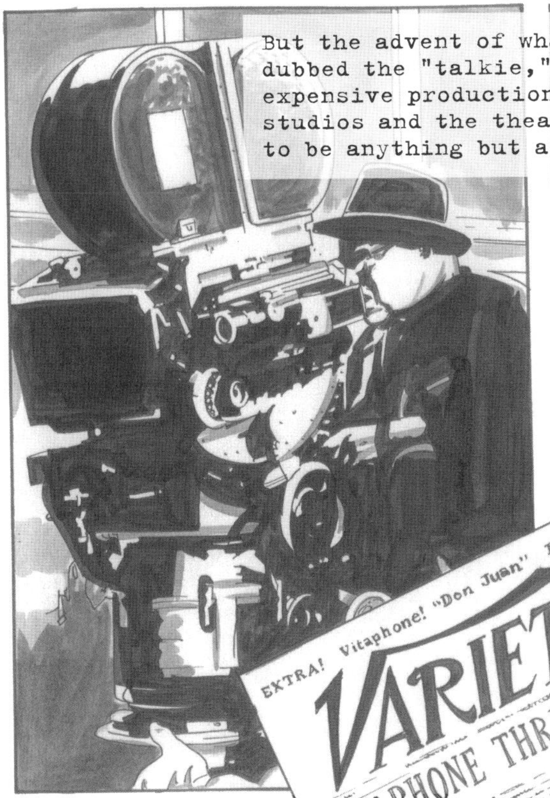
But the advent of what would come to be dubbed the "talkie," despite extremely expensive production costs by both the studios and the theatre owners, proved to be anything but a passing fad.

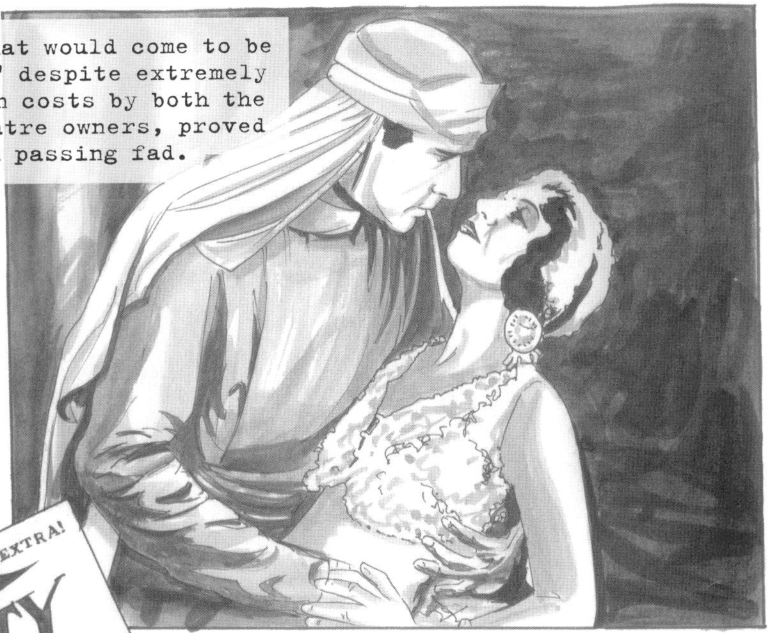

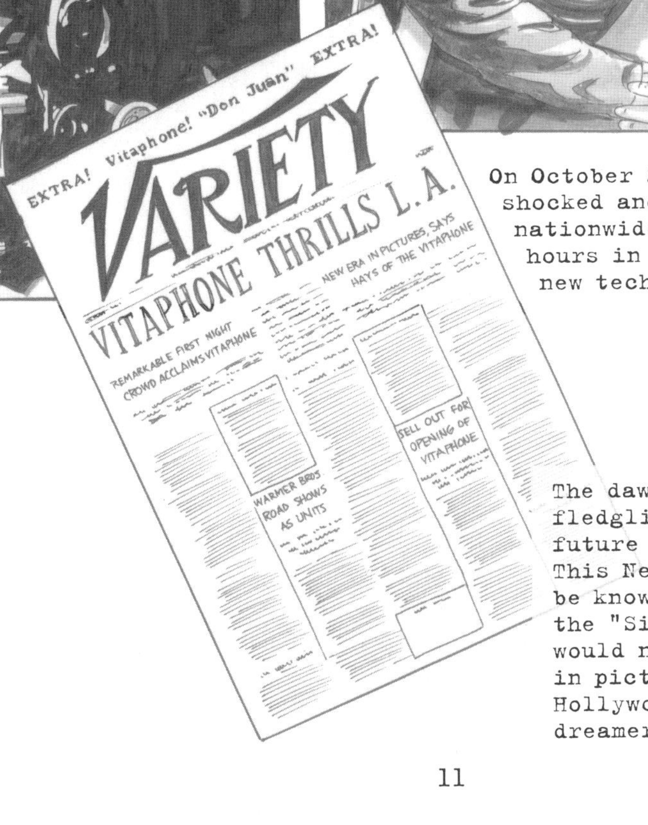
EXTRA! Vitaphone! "Don Juan" EXTRA!
VARIETY
VITAPHONE THRILLS L.A.
NEW ERA IN PICTURES, SAYS HAYS OF THE VITAPHONE
REMARKABLE FIRST NIGHT CROWD ACCLAIMS VITAPHONE
SELL OUT FOR OPENING OF VITAPHONE
WARMER BROS ROAD SHOWS AS UNITS

On October 26, 1926, the Vitaphone shocked and thrilled audiences nationwide. People lined up for hours in hopes of witnessing this new technological miracle.

The dawn of a New Era was upon the fledgling film industry, and the future looked even brighter, indeed. This New Era, which would come to be known to future generations as the "Silver Age" of film history, would not only give birth to sound in pictures, but also to some of Hollywood's greatest visionaries, dreamers, and legends.

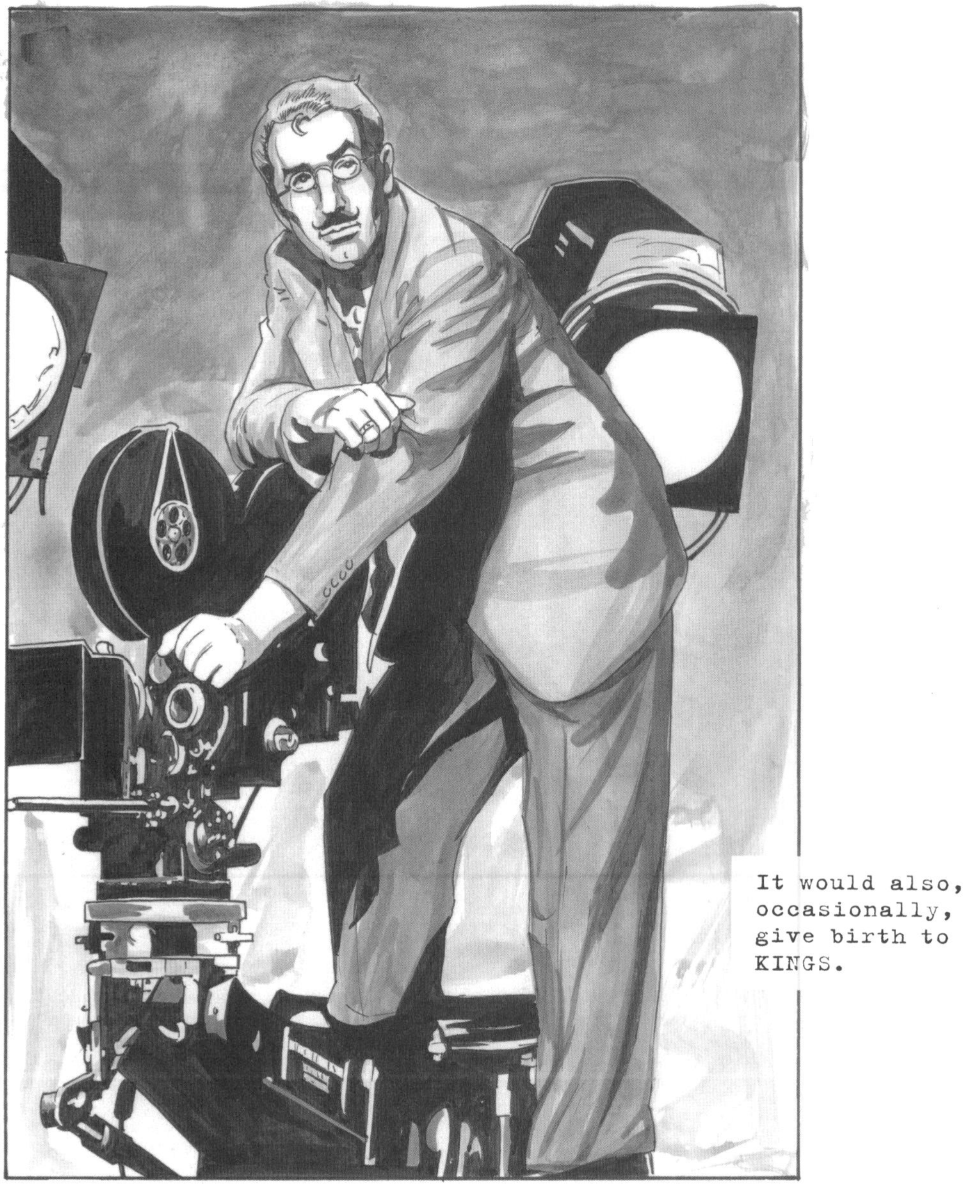
It would also, occasionally, give birth to KINGS.

KINGS

Reginald Desmond Walters
was born on March 3, 1896.

He would immediately be
nicknamed "Dizzy" by his
mother, because of the
frequent spells of light-
headedness she suffered
throughout the pregnancy.

The nickname would stick,
and soon Reginald Desmond
Walters would be known by
all as DIZZY WALTERS.

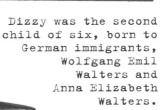

Dizzy was the second
child of six, born to
German immigrants,
Wolfgang Emil
Walters and
Anna Elizabeth
Walters.

The Walters
were a close-
knit family
that lived in
the small
rural town of
Hales Corners,
Ohio.

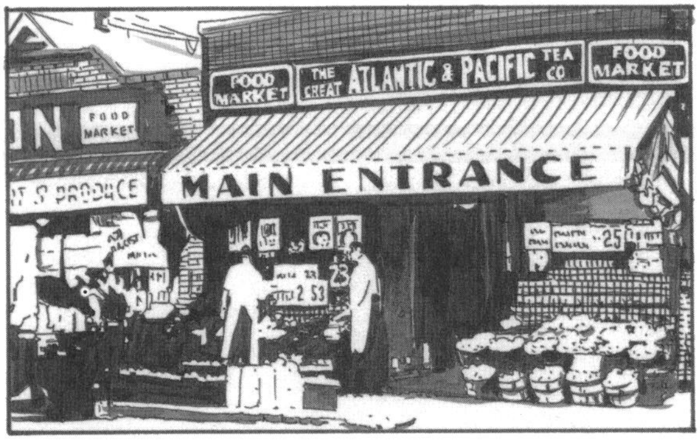
FOOD MARKET
THE GREAT ATLANTIC & PACIFIC TEA CO
FOOD MARKET
FOOD MARKET
MAIN ENTRANCE

Dizzy's father, Wolfgang, owned a small food market where all the family would be put to work. Dizzy discovered early on that, although the work was honest and the earnings respectable, his path lay elsewhere.

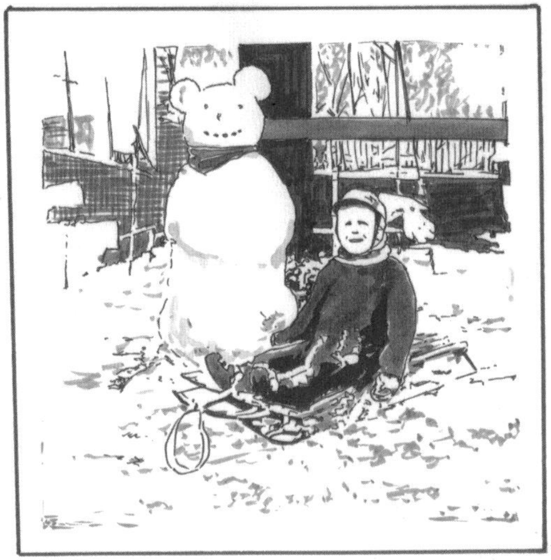

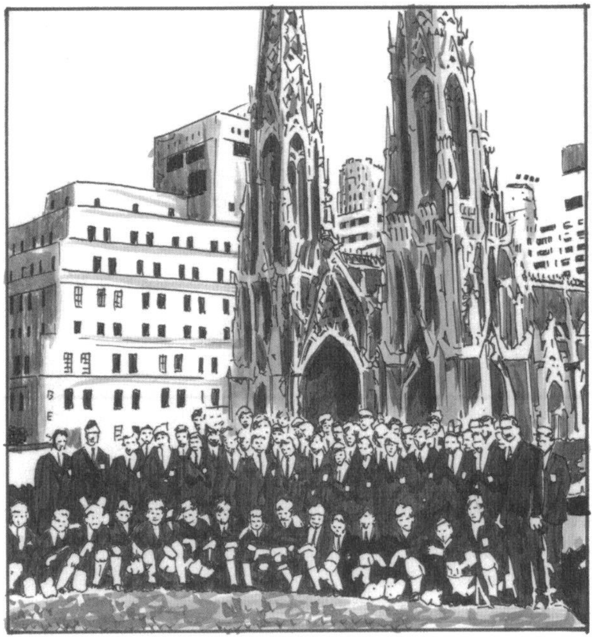

At age five, a young Dizzy Walters was enrolled at Saint Bonifay's School For Boys.

It was at Saint Bonifay's School For Boys that Dizzy was introduced to photography. Dizzy was instantly enthralled with working a camera. He frequently contributed his photographs to the school's newspaper, and eventually took over as Official Yearbook Photographer in his junior year.

Dizzy Walters would pass through high school with average grades. A classic underachiever, his teachers would constantly remark that Dizzy was a bright and gifted student, but that he didn't apply himself; he was a "daydreamer."

Sometime toward the end of his senior year, Dizzy joined a local amateur film troupe.

The group produced short, silent films which they would sometimes enter in contests and were occasionally shown at the local theatre as "lead-ins" for the feature presentations.

Although the group's films were rarely seen by an audience, and were paid little attention to when they were, Dizzy was not discouraged.

His path was clear now... His DESTINY.

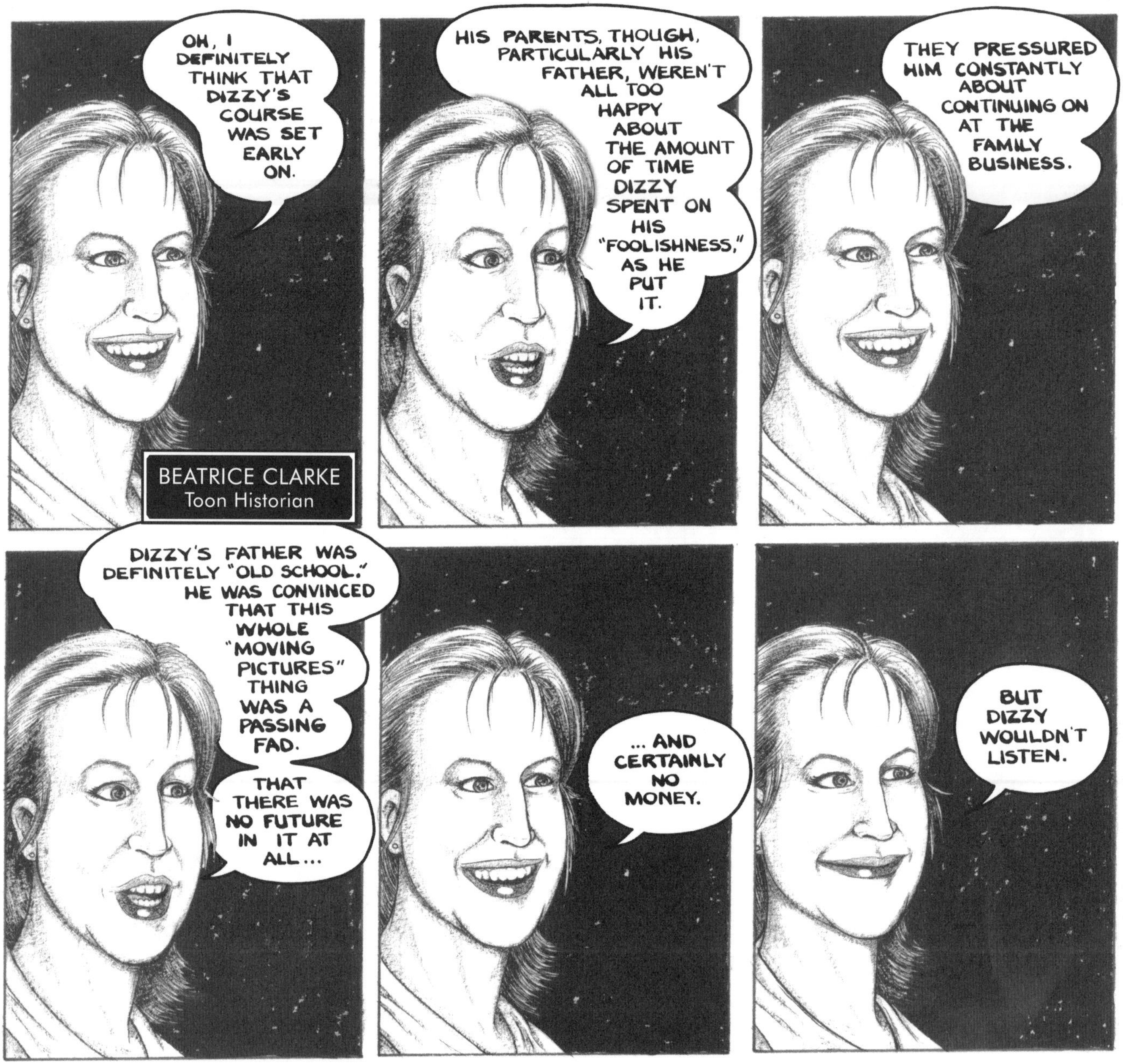
OH, I DEFINITELY THINK THAT DIZZY'S COURSE WAS SET EARLY ON.
BEATRICE CLARKE
Toon Historian
HIS PARENTS, THOUGH, PARTICULARLY HIS FATHER, WEREN'T ALL TOO HAPPY ABOUT THE AMOUNT OF TIME DIZZY SPENT ON HIS "FOOLISHNESS," AS HE PUT IT.
THEY PRESSURED HIM CONSTANTLY ABOUT CONTINUING ON AT THE FAMILY BUSINESS.
DIZZY'S FATHER WAS DEFINITELY "OLD SCHOOL." HE WAS CONVINCED THAT THIS WHOLE "MOVING PICTURES" THING WAS A PASSING FAD.
THAT THERE WAS NO FUTURE IN IT AT ALL...
... AND CERTAINLY NO MONEY.
BUT DIZZY WOULDN'T LISTEN.

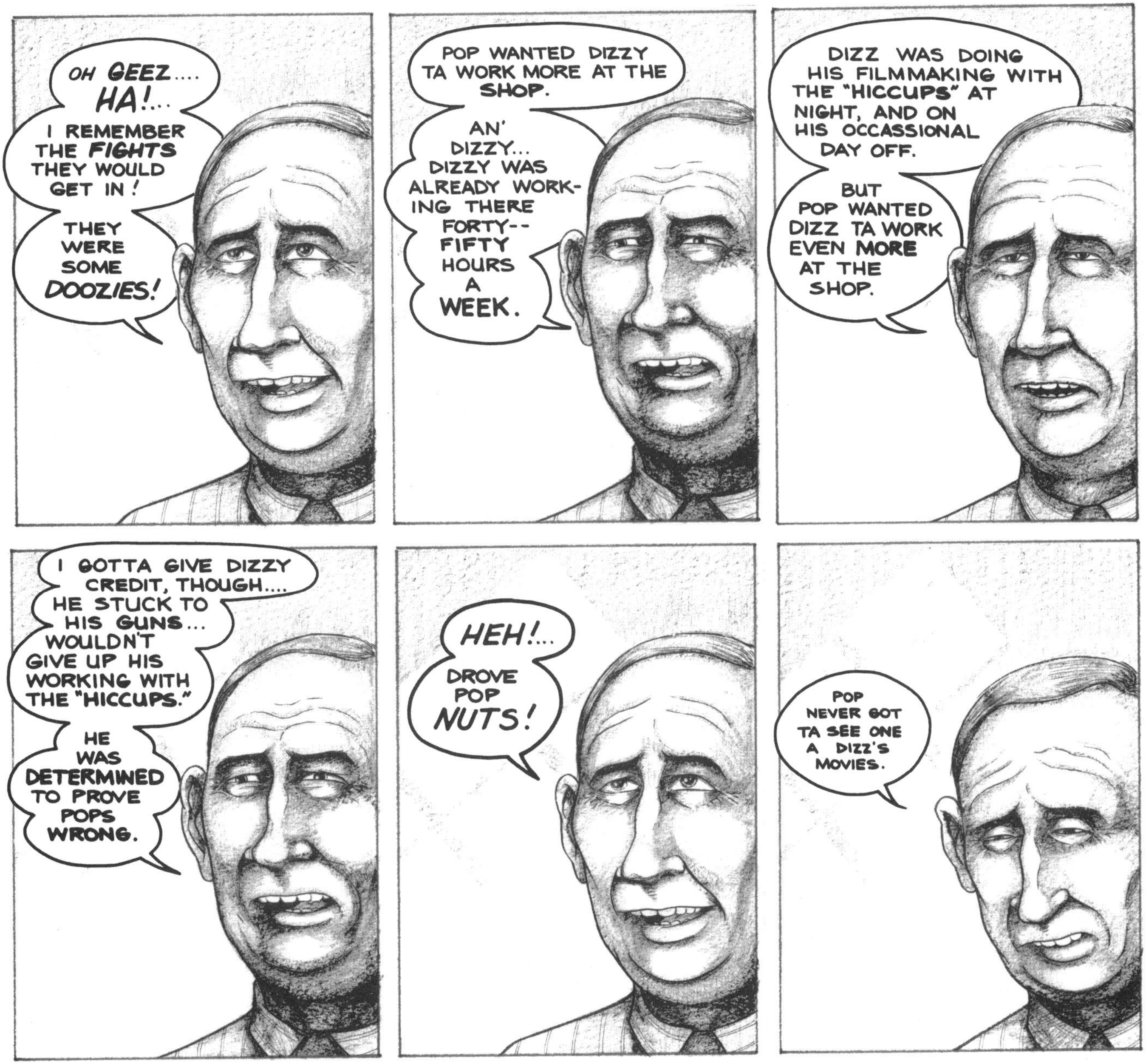
OH GEEZ.... HA!...
I REMEMBER THE FIGHTS THEY WOULD GET IN!
THEY WERE SOME DOOZIES!
POP WANTED DIZZY TA WORK MORE AT THE SHOP.
AN' DIZZY... DIZZY WAS ALREADY WORK-ING THERE FORTY-- FIFTY HOURS A WEEK.
DIZZ WAS DOING HIS FILMMAKING WITH THE "HICCUPS" AT NIGHT, AND ON HIS OCCASSIONAL DAY OFF.
BUT POP WANTED DIZZ TA WORK EVEN MORE AT THE SHOP.
I GOTTA GIVE DIZZY CREDIT, THOUGH.... HE STUCK TO HIS GUNS... WOULDN'T GIVE UP HIS WORKING WITH THE "HICCUPS."
HE WAS DETERMINED TO PROVE POPS WRONG.
HEH!...
DROVE POP NUTS!
POP NEVER GOT TA SEE ONE A DIZZ'S MOVIES.

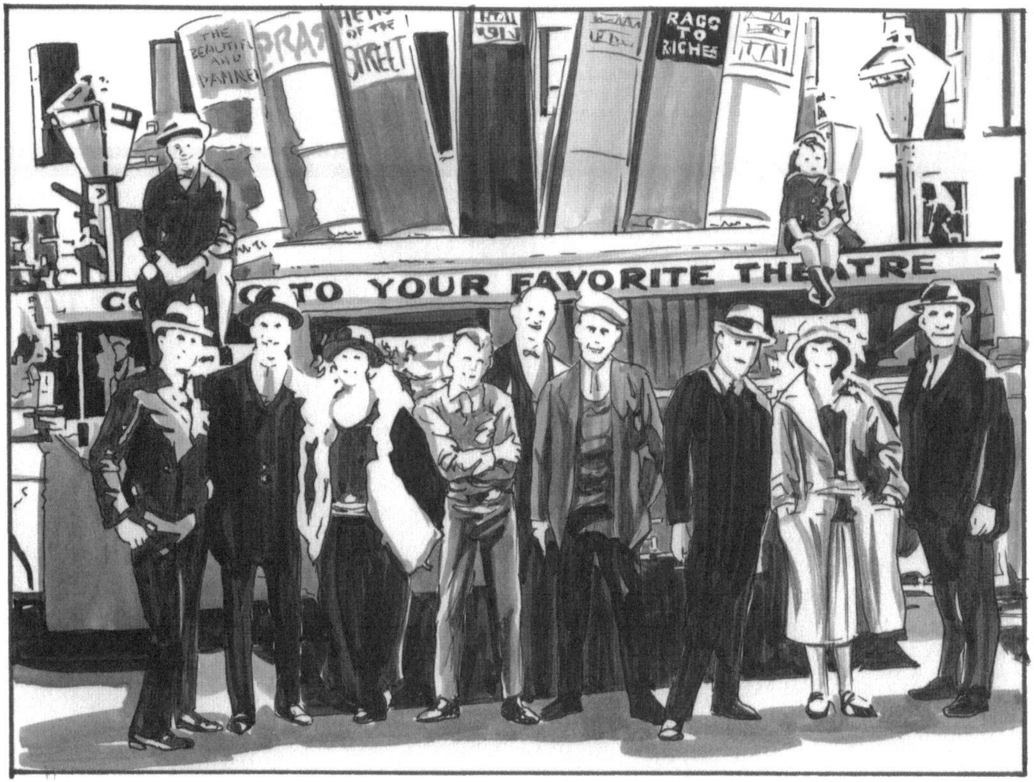
RAGS TO RICHES
OF THE STREET
TO YOUR FAVORITE THEATRE

The Hales Corners Camera Club, otherwise known as the "Hiccups," disbanded in 1921, only four years after it began. World War One was raging in Europe and several of the Hiccups members, including young Dizzy Walters, were called to serve their country.

After the war ended, Dizzy and one other original member of the Hiccups, Les Thordarson, would join a new group of filmmakers called the Ohio Players. Its members included two women, a teenager, and a nine-year-old boy. The group was a bit larger and more experienced than the Hiccups. It was also, unfortunately for Dizzy, located in the much larger city of Columbus, some seventy-five miles from Dizzy's hometown. The drive back and forth, coupled with working at the family store, eventually proved too much for Dizzy and forced some hard decisions.

Decisions that would prove to be both fortunate and costly.

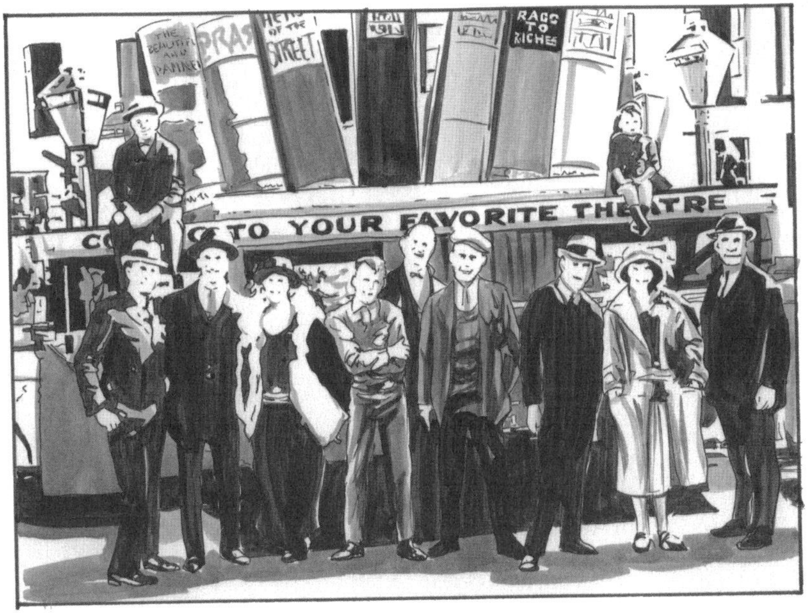
RAGS TO RICHES
TO YOUR FAVORITE

Three and a half weeks shy of his twenty-second birthday, Dizzy Walters packed his bags and left his family's home, and his family's business.

He rented a room in a modest home located on the lower East Side of downtown Columbus. There he set up a small makeshift studio. To pay the rent, Dizzy worked as a waiter during the days and delivered flowers on weekends. Dizzy had little spare time for his filmmaking, but still somehow managed to work six nights a week with the Ohio Players.

The Ohio Players managed to produce several short, low-budget features that played regionally to dozens of theatre audiences and received several favorable reviews. The group had a real "energy" to it, and although the group made no real profits from their films, Dizzy was thrilled with its modest successes.

His happiness would prove to be short-lived.

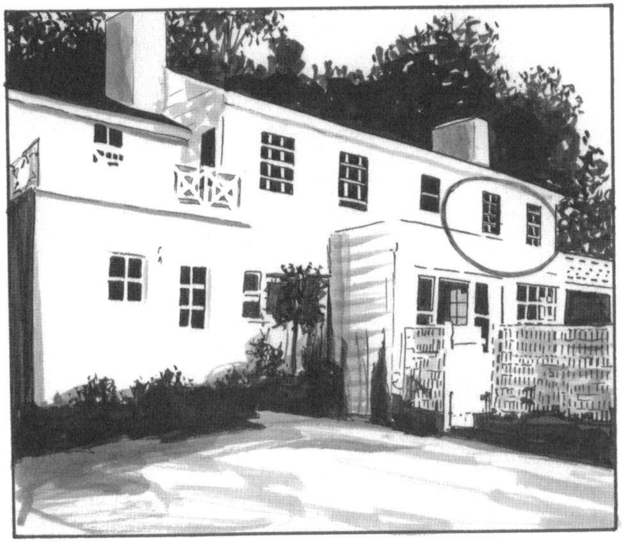

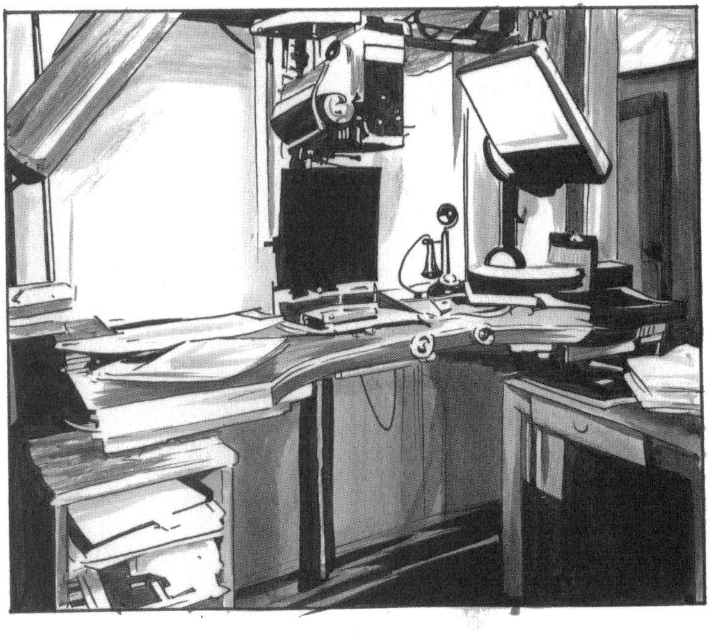

After just fourteen months with the Ohio Players, Dizzy Walters was frustrated. He felt that the Players' films were doing okay, but that they weren't moving forward... That they weren't progressing quickly enough. Dizzy felt that the films "lacked something"-- That they were just producing "more of the same." They needed a "hook."

Although Dizzy continued on with the Ohio Players, he spent less and less time with them.

Dizzy could be found spending more of his free time at the local bars and nightclubs.

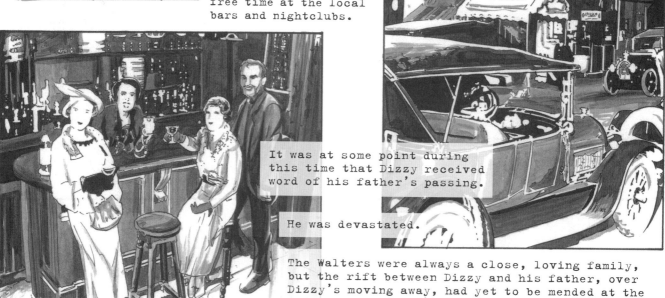

It was at some point during this time that Dizzy received word of his father's passing.

He was devastated.

The Walters were always a close, loving family, but the rift between Dizzy and his father, over Dizzy's moving away, had yet to be mended at the time of his father's death.

Dizzy began to drink heavily.

He would later refer to this period of his life as his "Dark Days."

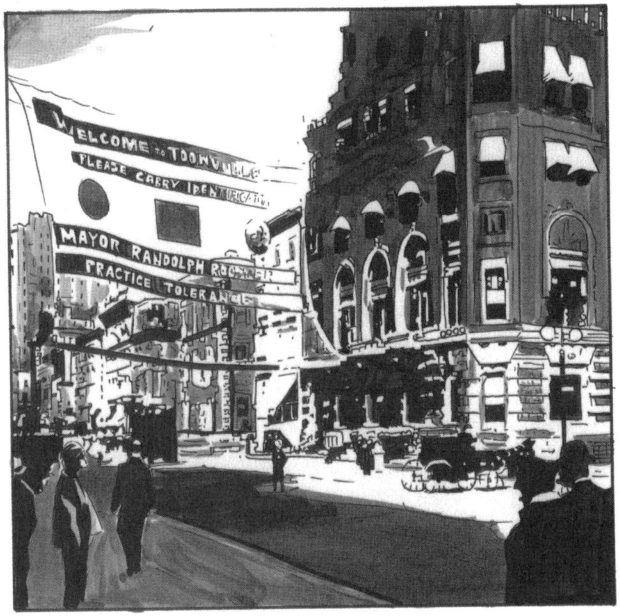
WELCOME TO
MAYOR RANDOLPH
PRACTICE TOLERANCE

Dizzy's heavy drinking would take him through Dark Days and down Dark Paths. He began finding himself in seedier and seedier parts of town, until finally-- one night-- he found himself wandering through the dark streets of the heavily segregated part of the city known as "TOONSVILLE"-- An area almost exclusively inhabited by very poor Toons.

It was in Toonsville that Dizzy stumbled upon a back-alley night-club, where he heard the sound of piano music-- GOOD piano music-- coming from within.

Dizzy would open the doors and step inside that seedy nightclub, and take his first steps down the path into history...

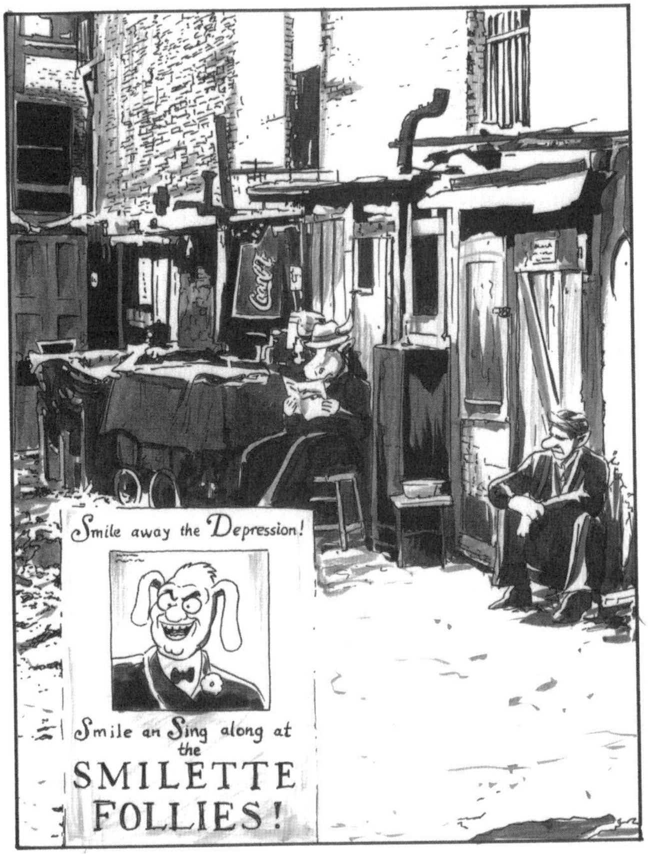
Smile away the Depression!
Smile an Sing along at the
SMILETTE FOLLIES!

And the RAT that sat at the piano would lead Dizzy
down that path... The path to the kingdom known as
Hollywood... and TOGETHER, they would come to
RULE that kingdom!

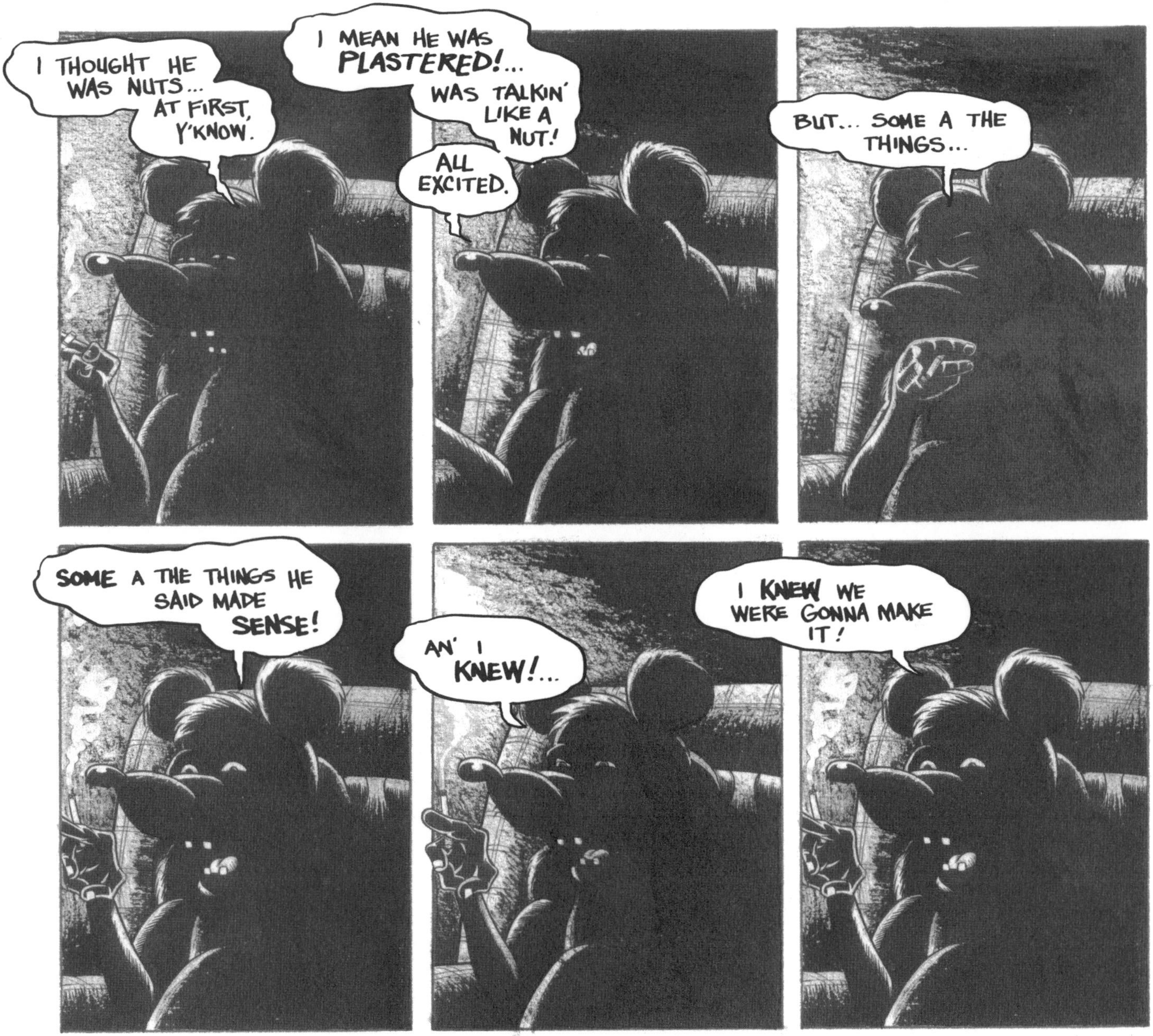
I THOUGHT HE WAS NUTS... AT FIRST, Y'KNOW.
I MEAN HE WAS PLASTERED!...
WAS TALKIN' LIKE A NUT!
ALL EXCITED.
BUT... SOME A THE THINGS...
SOME A THE THINGS HE SAID MADE SENSE!
AN' I KNEW!...
I KNEW WE WERE GONNA MAKE IT!

IN THE BEGINNING

The moment that Dizzy Walters and Rickey Rat met, there was MAGIC... An almost instantaneous connection.

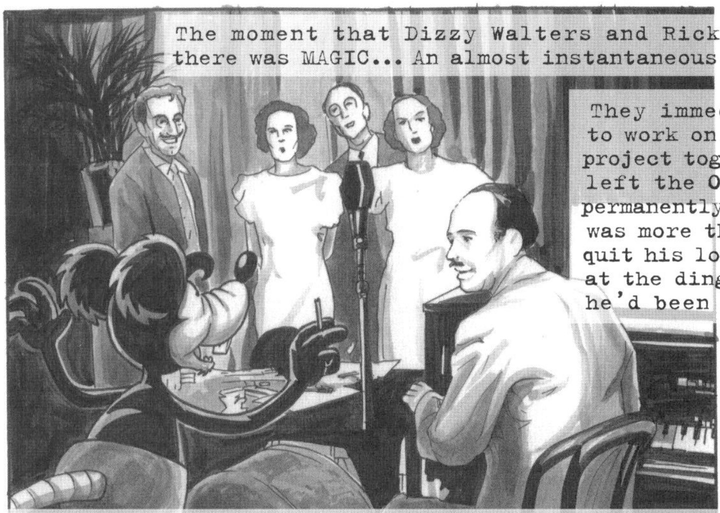

They immediately set to work on their first project together. Dizzy left the Ohio Players permanently, and Rickey was more than happy to quit his low-paying gig at the dingy nightclub he'd been working at.

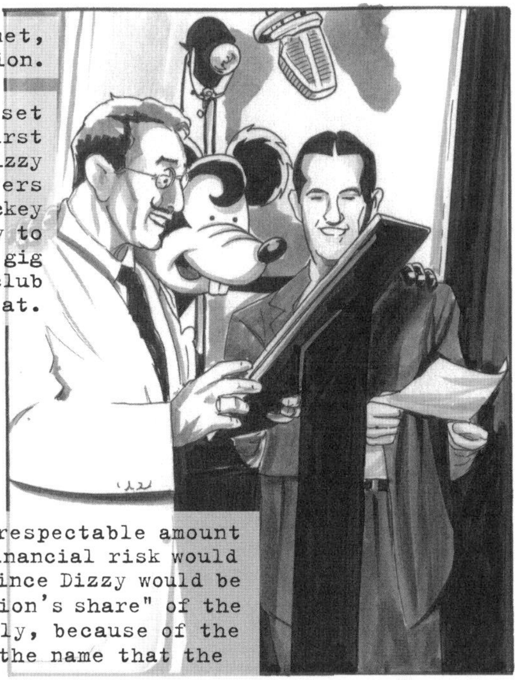

Rickey was broke, but Dizzy had managed to save a somewhat respectable amount of money from waiting tables. Dizzy assured Rickey that the financial risk would be solely Dizzy's responsibility. It was further agreed that since Dizzy would be solely shouldering the financial risks, he should reap the "lion's share" of the profits, should their endeavor prove successful. Additionally, because of the financial situation and existing prejudices against Toons, the name that the production company would be called was "DIZZY WALTERS STUDIOS."

Being a Toon, and fully realizing the limited opportunities that toons had back then, Rickey eagerly agreed to the terms.

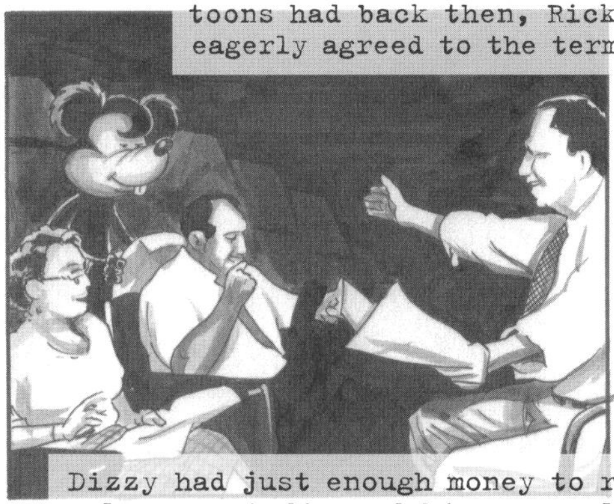

Dizzy had just enough money to rent a larger studio and hire a small, part-time crew. During the early production period, it became quite evident to all that they were onto something... Something SPECIAL.

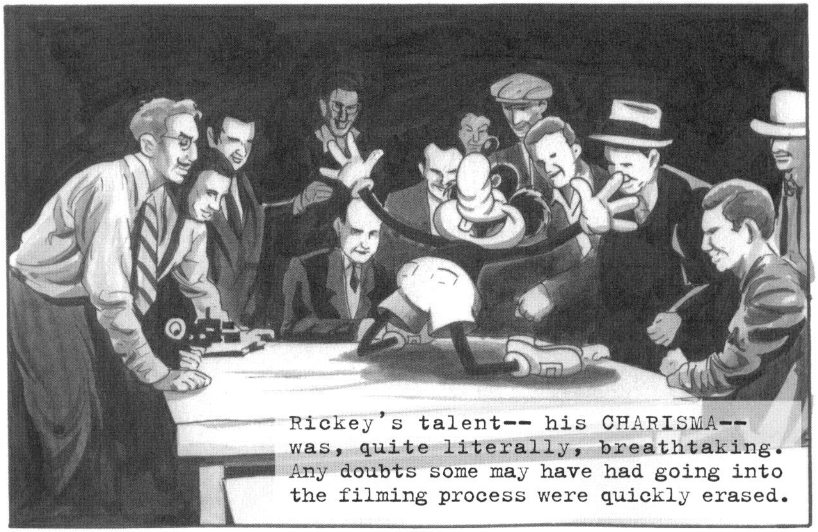

Rickey's talent-- his CHARISMA-- was, quite literally, breathtaking. Any doubts some may have had going into the filming process were quickly erased.

With the filming of their first project completed, Dizzy and Rickey packed up, leaving their homes in Columbus, and headed West to Hollywood. Along the way, they stopped and picked up Dizzy's younger brother, Rog. Dizzy had, through a series of letters, convinced Rog to accompany him and Rickey, and join them in their endeavor. Rog, who had been growing restless running the family business, was desperately looking for a change.

He readily agreed.

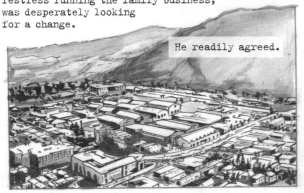

Once in Hollywood, Dizzy used his few remaining funds, and a few bucks he borrowed from Rog, to rent a small office from which they intended to distribute their film.

He then commissioned several inexperienced, but very eager, salesmen to sell the film to the theatres. Dizzy was broke and the salesmen he signed up were desperate-- and they were all having the times of their lives.

Through persistence, sheer luck, and promises to the theatre owners that Dizzy wasn't really sure he could ever fulfill, they managed to have the film shown at a prominent Hollywood theatre.

"RAILROAD RICKEY," Dizzy Walters' first, and to date, only feature film, was about to make its debut to the viewing public.

Only one question remained...
WERE THE AMERICAN AUDIENCES READY
TO ACCEPT A TOON IN MOTION PICTURES?

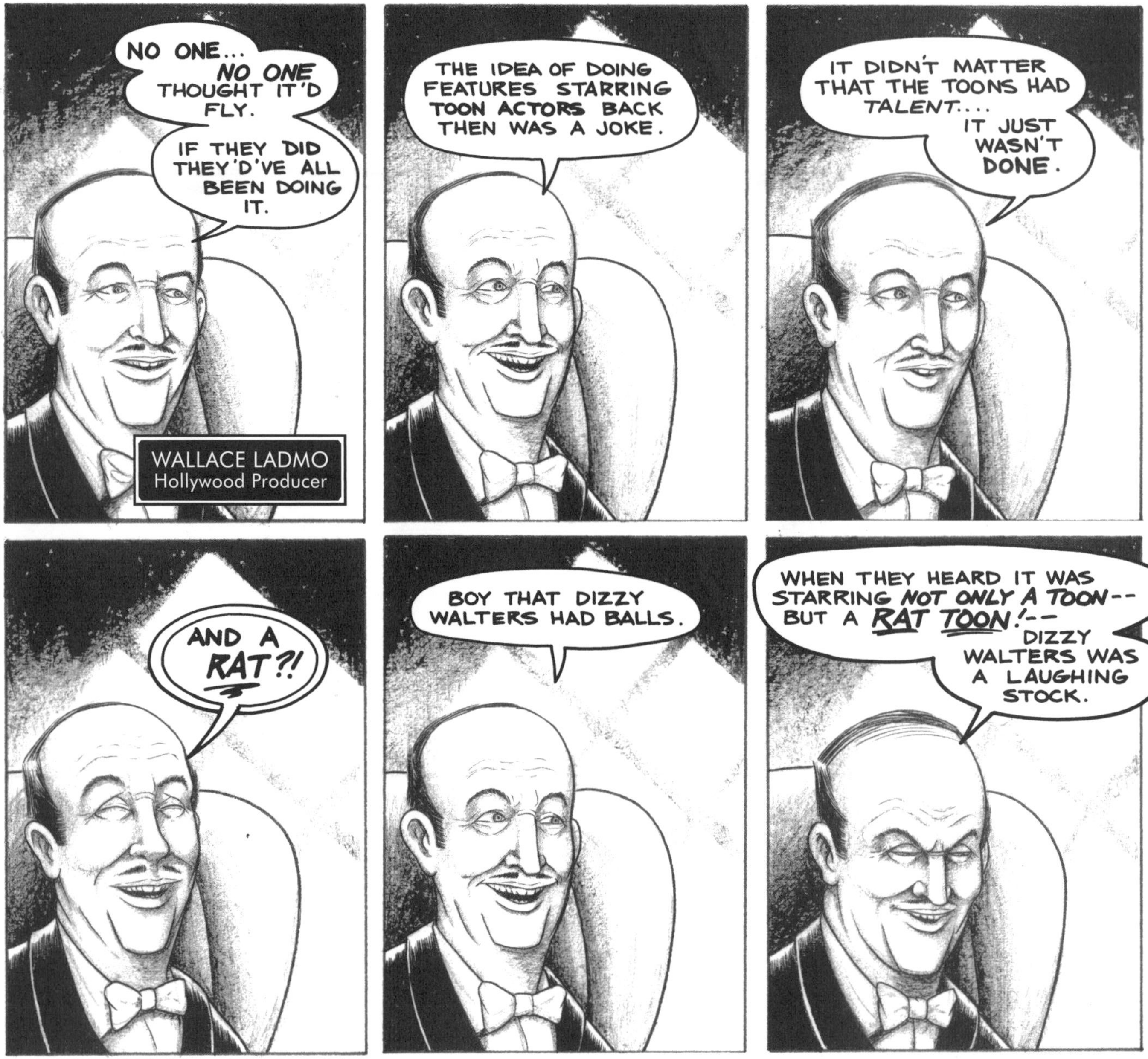
NO ONE... NO ONE THOUGHT IT'D FLY.
IF THEY DID THEY'D'VE ALL BEEN DOING IT.
WALLACE LADMO
Hollywood Producer
THE IDEA OF DOING FEATURES STARRING TOON ACTORS BACK THEN WAS A JOKE.
IT DIDN'T MATTER THAT THE TOONS HAD TALENT....
IT JUST WASN'T DONE.
AND A RAT?!
BOY THAT DIZZY WALTERS HAD BALLS.
WHEN THEY HEARD IT WAS STARRING NOT ONLY A TOON-- BUT A RAT TOON!--
DIZZY WALTERS WAS A LAUGHING STOCK.

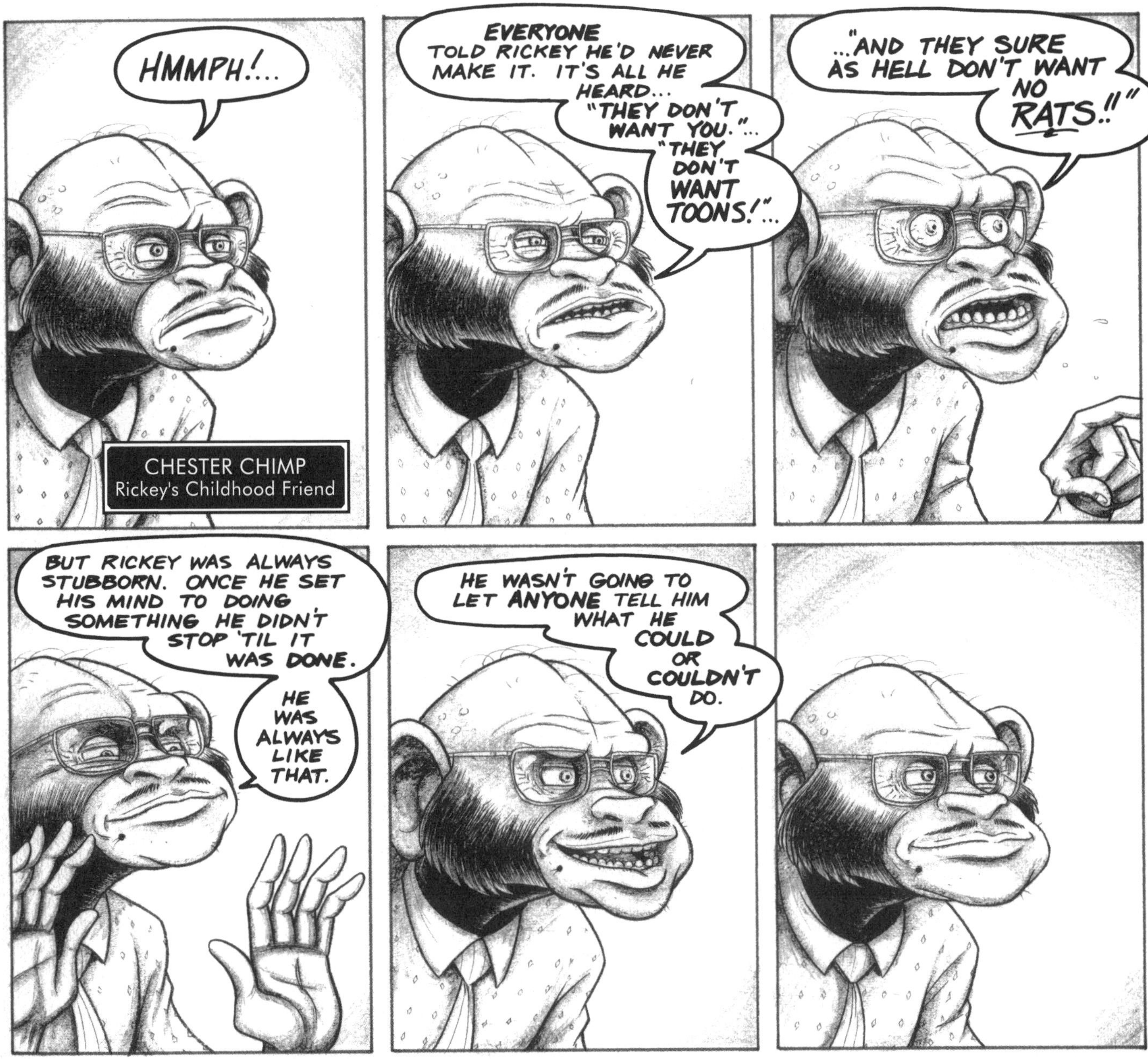
HMMPH!...
CHESTER CHIMP
Rickey's Childhood Friend
EVERYONE TOLD RICKEY HE'D NEVER MAKE IT. IT'S ALL HE HEARD... "THEY DON'T WANT YOU."... "THEY DON'T WANT TOONS!"...
..."AND THEY SURE AS HELL DON'T WANT NO RATS!!"
BUT RICKEY WAS ALWAYS STUBBORN. ONCE HE SET HIS MIND TO DOING SOMETHING HE DIDN'T STOP 'TIL IT WAS DONE.
HE WAS ALWAYS LIKE THAT.
HE WASN'T GOING TO LET ANYONE TELL HIM WHAT HE COULD OR COULDN'T DO.

OH YEAH... ALL MY TOON PALS USED TA LAUGH AT ME WHEN I TOLD 'EM I WAS GONNA BE IN PICTURES.
BUT I SHOWED 'EM.

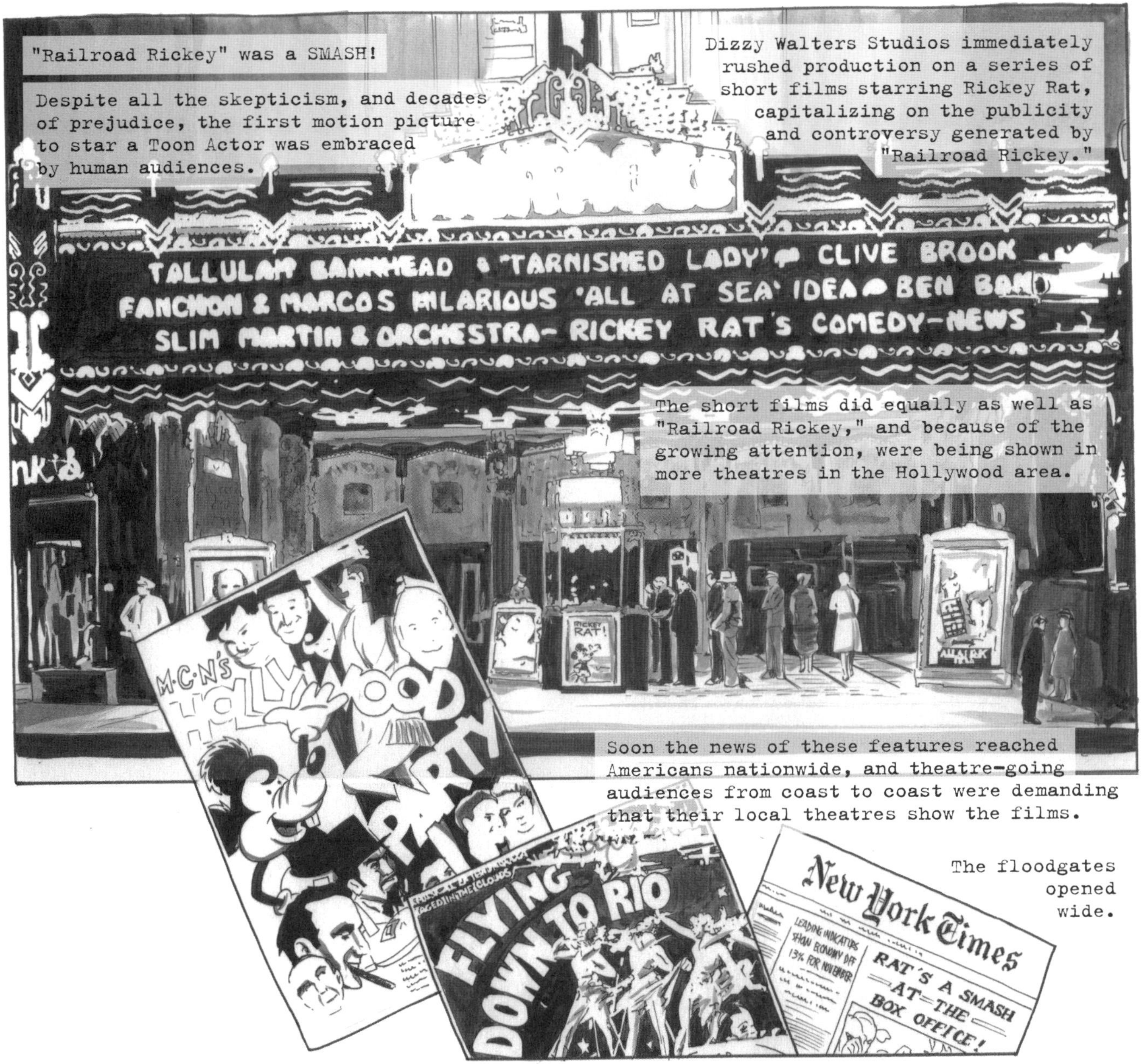
"Railroad Rickey" was a SMASH!
Despite all the skepticism, and decades of prejudice, the first motion picture to star a Toon Actor was embraced by human audiences.
Dizzy Walters Studios immediately rushed production on a series of short films starring Rickey Rat, capitalizing on the publicity and controversy generated by "Railroad Rickey."
TALLULAH BANKHEAD & "TARNISHED LADY" CLIVE BROOK
FANCHON & MARCOS HILARIOUS 'ALL AT SEA' IDEA BEN BA
SLIM MARTIN & ORCHESTRA- RICKEY RAT'S COMEDY-NEWS
The short films did equally as well as "Railroad Rickey," and because of the growing attention, were being shown in more theatres in the Hollywood area.
RICKEY RAT!
M-G-N's HOLLYWOOD PARTY
Soon the news of these features reached Americans nationwide, and theatre-going audiences from coast to coast were demanding that their local theatres show the films.
FLYING DOWN TO RIO
The floodgates opened wide.
New York Times
LEADING INDICATORS SHOW ECONOMY OFF 13% FOR NOVEMBER
RAT'S A SMASH AT THE BOX OFFICE!

Quickly, all the major motion picture studios began producing films starring Toon Actors. Six months after the debut of "Railroad Rickey," four major studios would release full-length features starring entirely Toon casts.

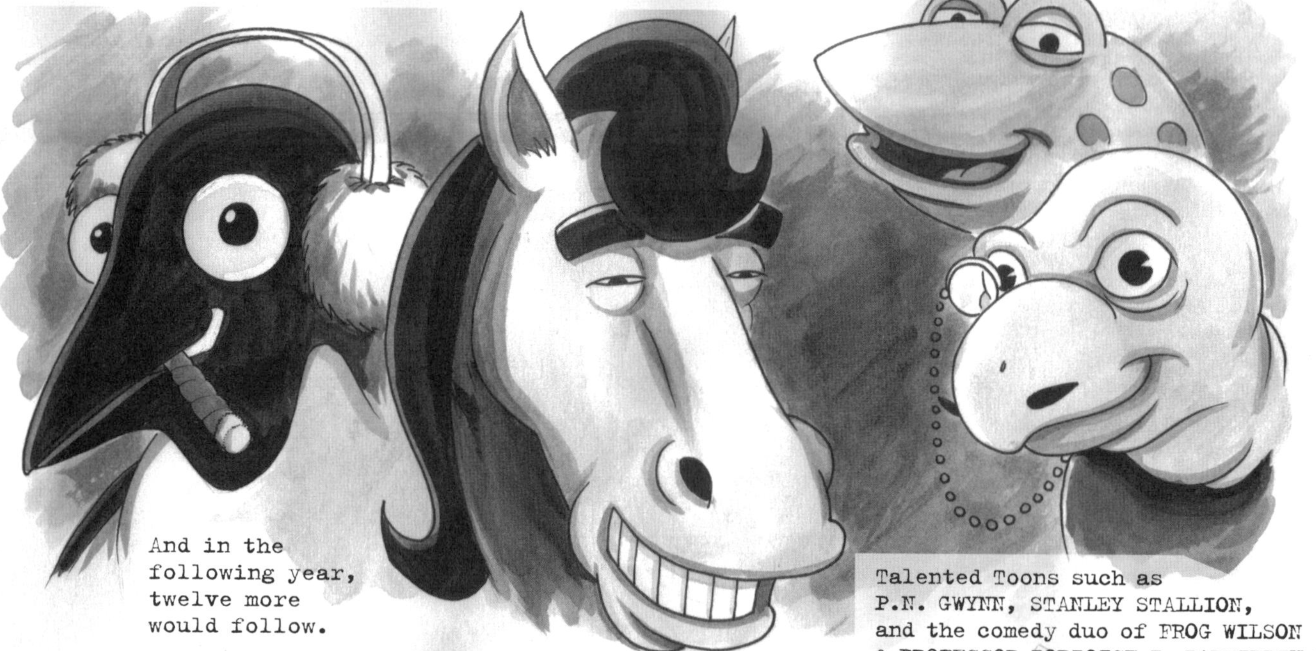

And in the following year, twelve more would follow.

Talented Toons such as P.N. GWYNN, STANLEY STALLION, and the comedy duo of FROG WILSON & PROFESSOR TORTOISE T. TARMILLIUM made their cinematic debuts.

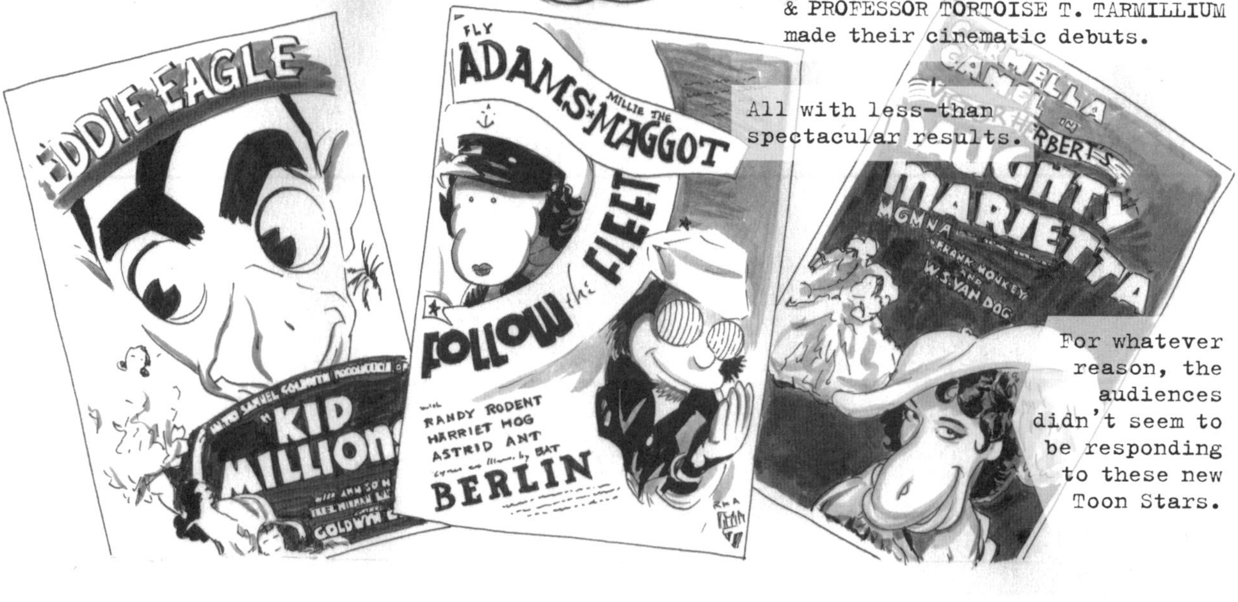
EDDIE EAGLE
KID MILLIONS
FLY
ADAMS
MILLIE THE MAGGOT
FOLLOW the FLEET
RANDY RODENT
HARRIET HOG
ASTRID ANT
BERLIN
MARIETTA
FRANK MONKEY
W.S. VAN DOG

All with less-than spectacular results.

For whatever reason, the audiences didn't seem to be responding to these new Toon Stars.

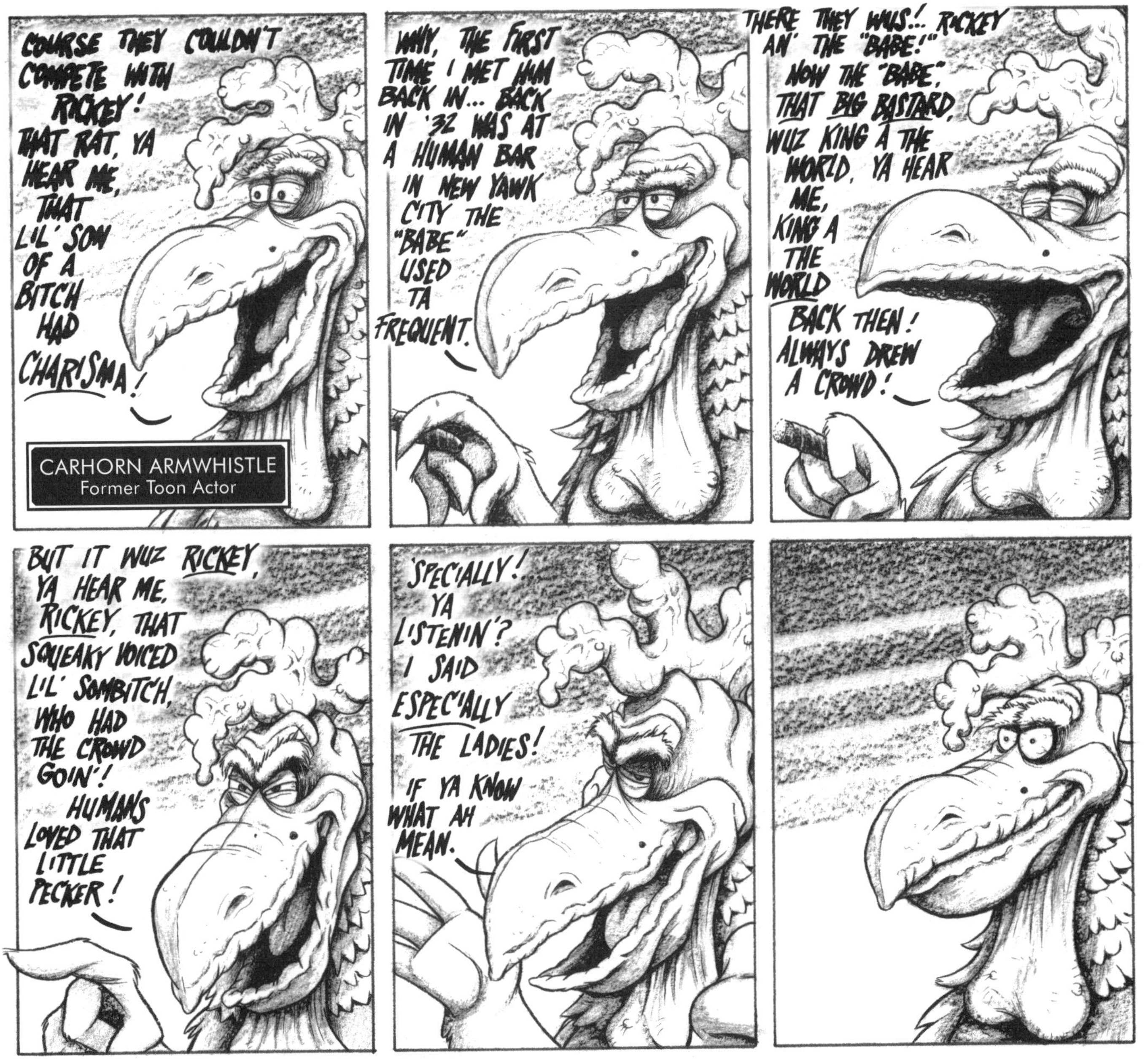
COURSE THEY COULDN'T COMPETE WITH RICKEY! THAT RAT, YA HEAR ME, THAT LIL' SON OF A BITCH HAD CHARISMA!
CARHORN ARMWHISTLE
Former Toon Actor
WHY, THE FIRST TIME I MET HIM BACK IN... BACK IN '32 WAS AT A HUMAN BAR IN NEW YAWK CITY THE "BABE" USED TA FREQUENT.
THERE THEY WUS!.. RICKEY AN' THE "BABE!"
NOW THE "BABE", THAT BIG BASTARD, WUZ KING A THE WORLD, YA HEAR ME, KING A THE WORLD BACK THEN!
ALWAYS DREW A CROWD!
BUT IT WUZ RICKEY, YA HEAR ME, RICKEY, THAT SQUEAKY VOICED LIL' SOMBITCH, WHO HAD THE CROWD GOIN'!
HUMANS LOVED THAT LITTLE PECKER!
'SPECIALLY! YA LISTENIN'? I SAID ESPECIALLY THE LADIES!
IF YA KNOW WHAT AH MEAN.

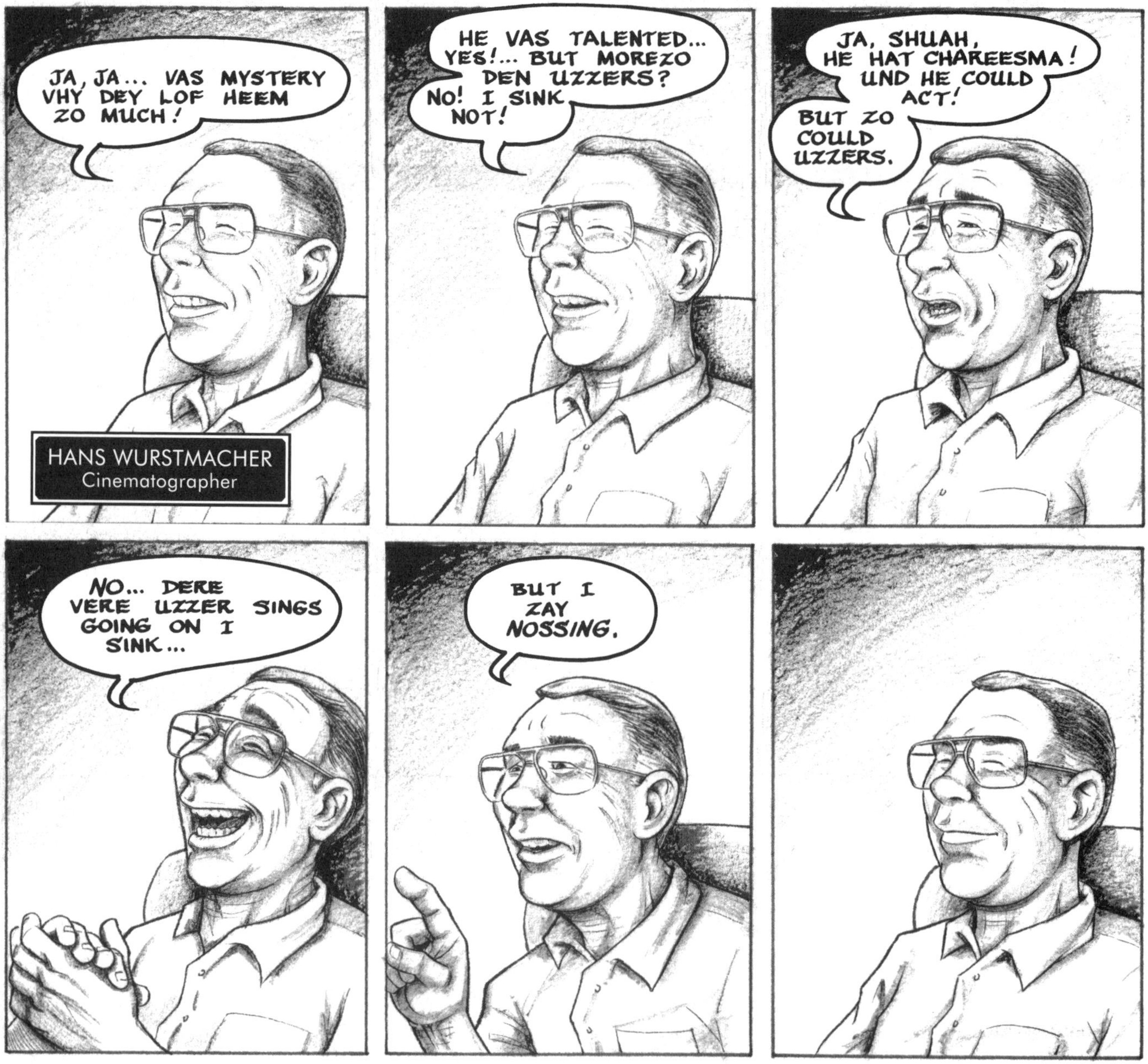
JA, JA... VAS MYSTERY VHY DEY LOF HEEM ZO MUCH!
HANS WURSTMACHER
Cinematographer
HE VAS TALENTED... YES!... BUT MOREZO DEN UZZERS?
NO! I SINK NOT!
JA, SHUAH, HE HAT CHAREESMA! UND HE COULD ACT!
BUT ZO COULD UZZERS.
NO... DERE VERE UZZER SINGS GOING ON I SINK...
BUT I ZAY *NOSSING*.

WELL ... HRRM! ... WELL ... >AHEM< ... WELL YES, ...

PORTLY PIG
Former Toon Star

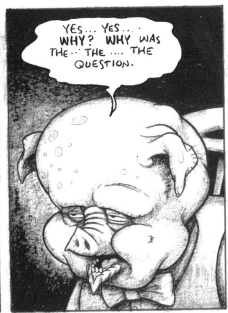

YES ... YES .... WHY? WHY WAS THE ... THE .... THE QUESTION.

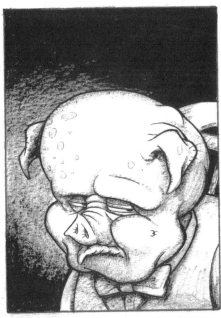

NO ONE ... NO ONE ... NO ONE ... SEEMED TO HAVE THE ANSWER.

AHAAHGHK! GHAA!.. CUHAOOOCH!...

HAROOM! HRRM!... HH!

39

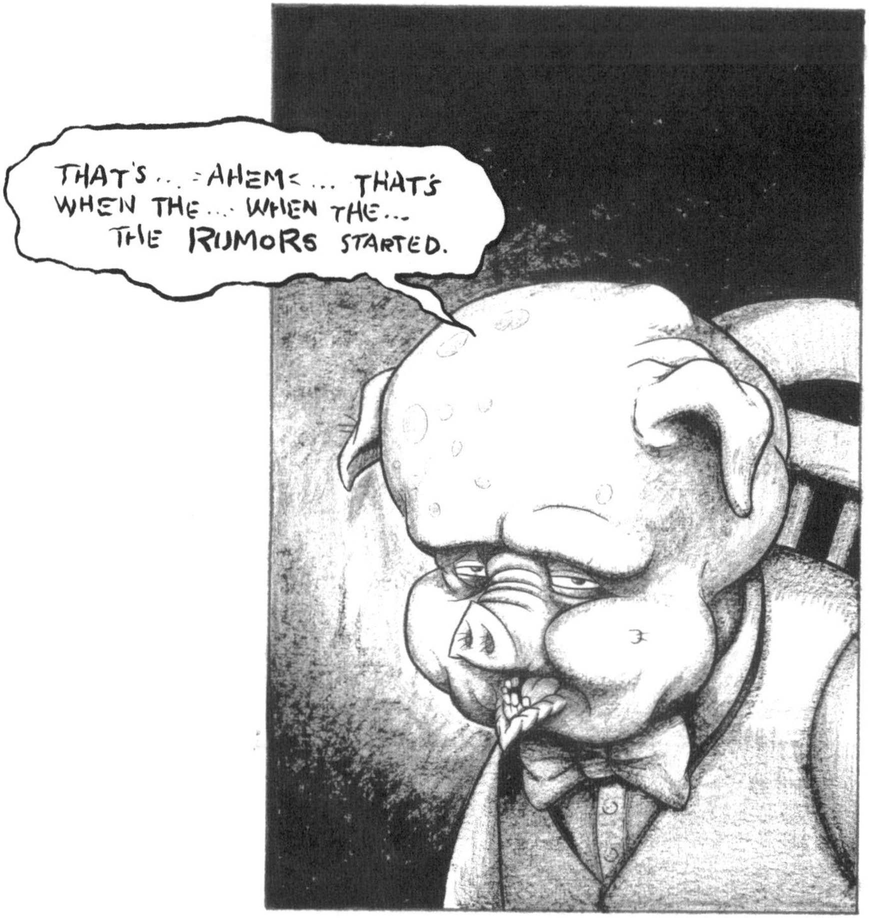
THAT'S... =AHEM= ... THAT'S WHEN THE... WHEN THE... THE RUMORS STARTED.

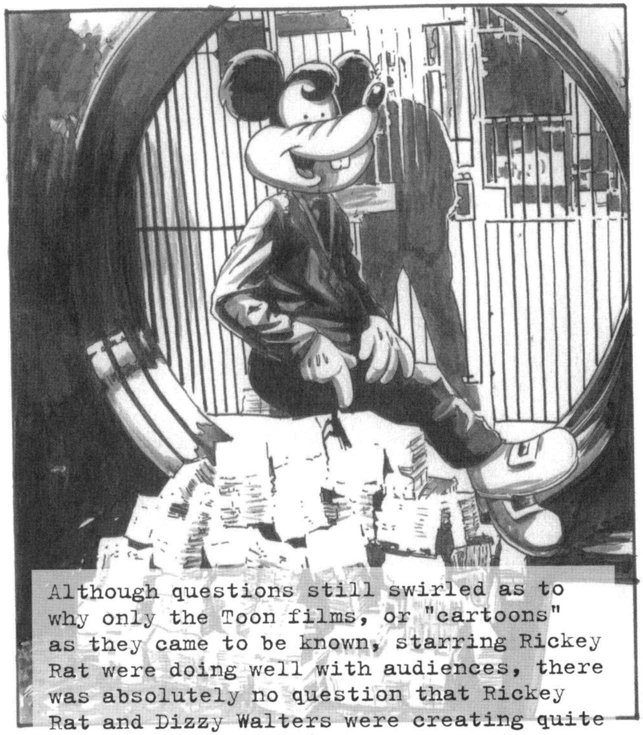

Although questions still swirled as to why only the Toon films, or "cartoons" as they came to be known, starring Rickey Rat were doing well with audiences, there was absolutely no question that Rickey Rat and Dizzy Walters were creating quite a stir in Hollywood's inner circles.

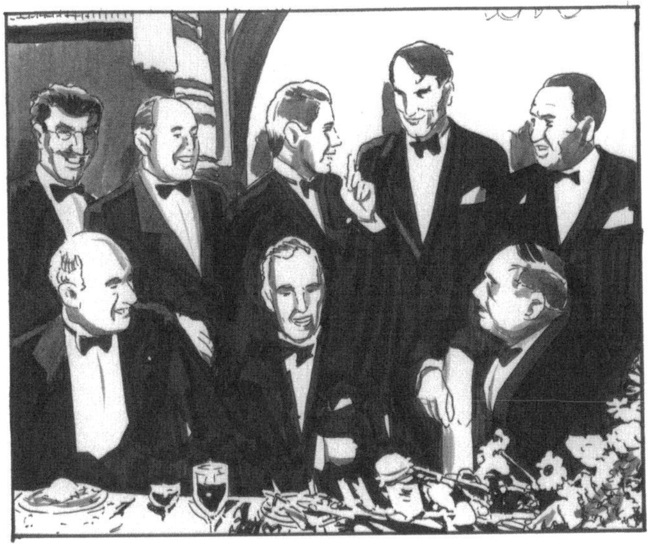

Both quickly became Hollywood "A-Listers," and the popular duo now found themselves rubbing elbows with Hollywood's elite.

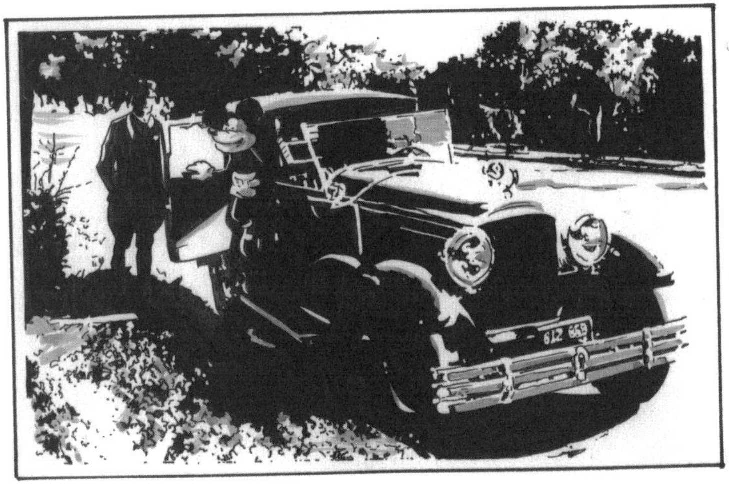

And the money was pouring in.

Production stepped up at Dizzy Walters Studios and plans for features, starring several new Toons, were being made. It was agreed, by Dizzy and his new team of filmmakers, that Rickey needed a female counterpart-- a romantic interest-- to spice up the new films.

MILLIE MARSUPIAL was signed for the role. A "Blonde Toon Bombshell" with stage acting and singing credentials. Rickey and Millie would star together in the next two Dizzy Walters Studio productions, with mixed results. It was agreed by all who saw the films that they were good, and that there was some nice chemistry between Rickey and Millie, but again, the audiences responded more to Rickey.

Hopeful Toon Actors were becoming more and more concerned as to the reasons why human audiences were only responding to Rickey. Always a superstitious lot, Toons would tend to embrace the irrational, the unbelievable, when rational explanations failed.

Disturbing rumors were beginning to surface regarding Rickey's uncanny popularity, and Millie Marsupial would soon discover how brutal the business of moviemaking in Hollywood could be.

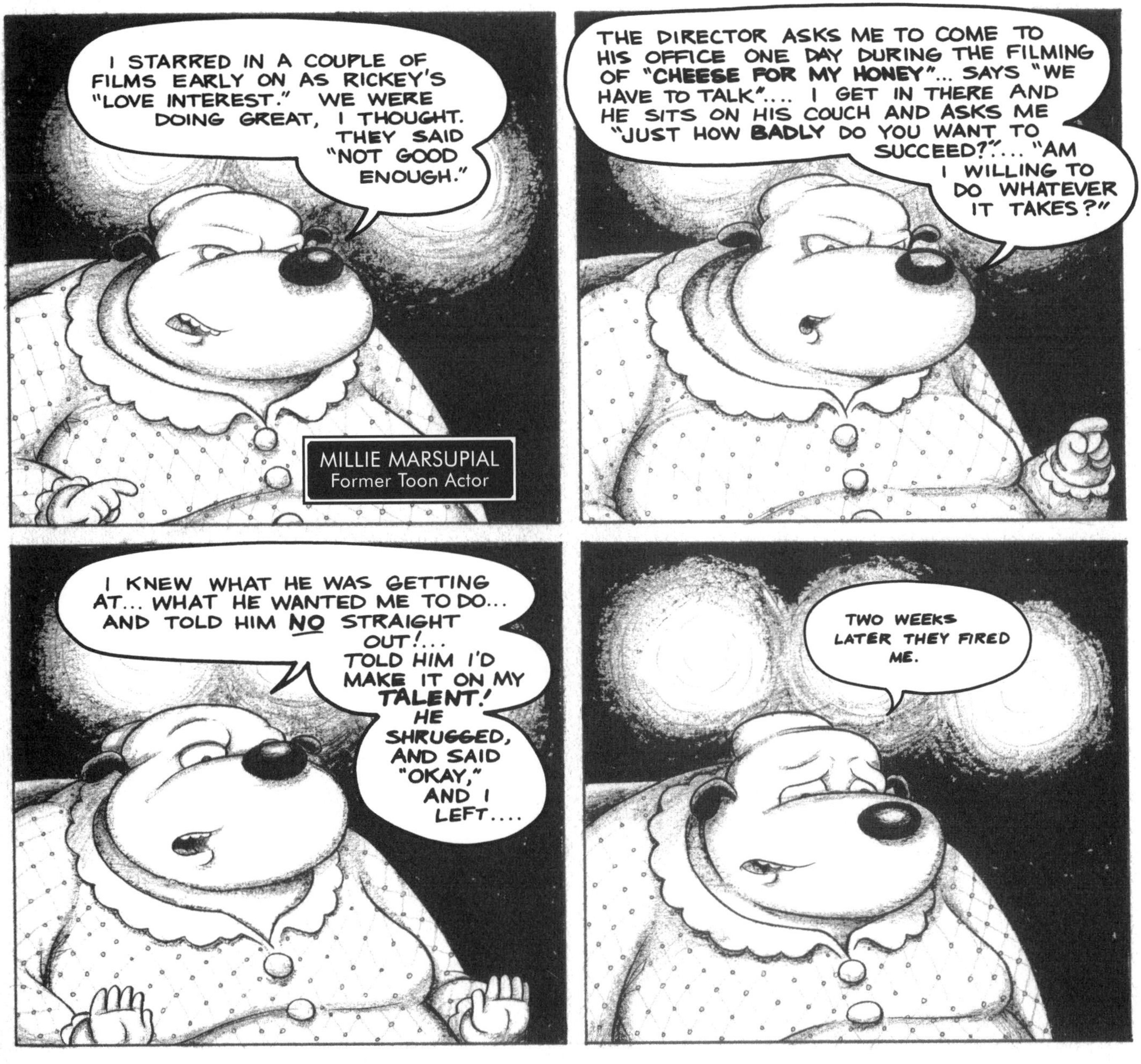
I STARRED IN A COUPLE OF FILMS EARLY ON AS RICKEY'S "LOVE INTEREST." WE WERE DOING GREAT, I THOUGHT. THEY SAID "NOT GOOD ENOUGH."
MILLIE MARSUPIAL
Former Toon Actor
THE DIRECTOR ASKS ME TO COME TO HIS OFFICE ONE DAY DURING THE FILMING OF "CHEESE FOR MY HONEY"... SAYS "WE HAVE TO TALK".... I GET IN THERE AND HE SITS ON HIS COUCH AND ASKS ME "JUST HOW BADLY DO YOU WANT TO SUCCEED?".... "AM I WILLING TO DO WHATEVER IT TAKES?"
I KNEW WHAT HE WAS GETTING AT... WHAT HE WANTED ME TO DO... AND TOLD HIM NO STRAIGHT OUT!... TOLD HIM I'D MAKE IT ON MY TALENT! HE SHRUGGED, AND SAID "OKAY," AND I LEFT....
TWO WEEKS LATER THEY FIRED ME.

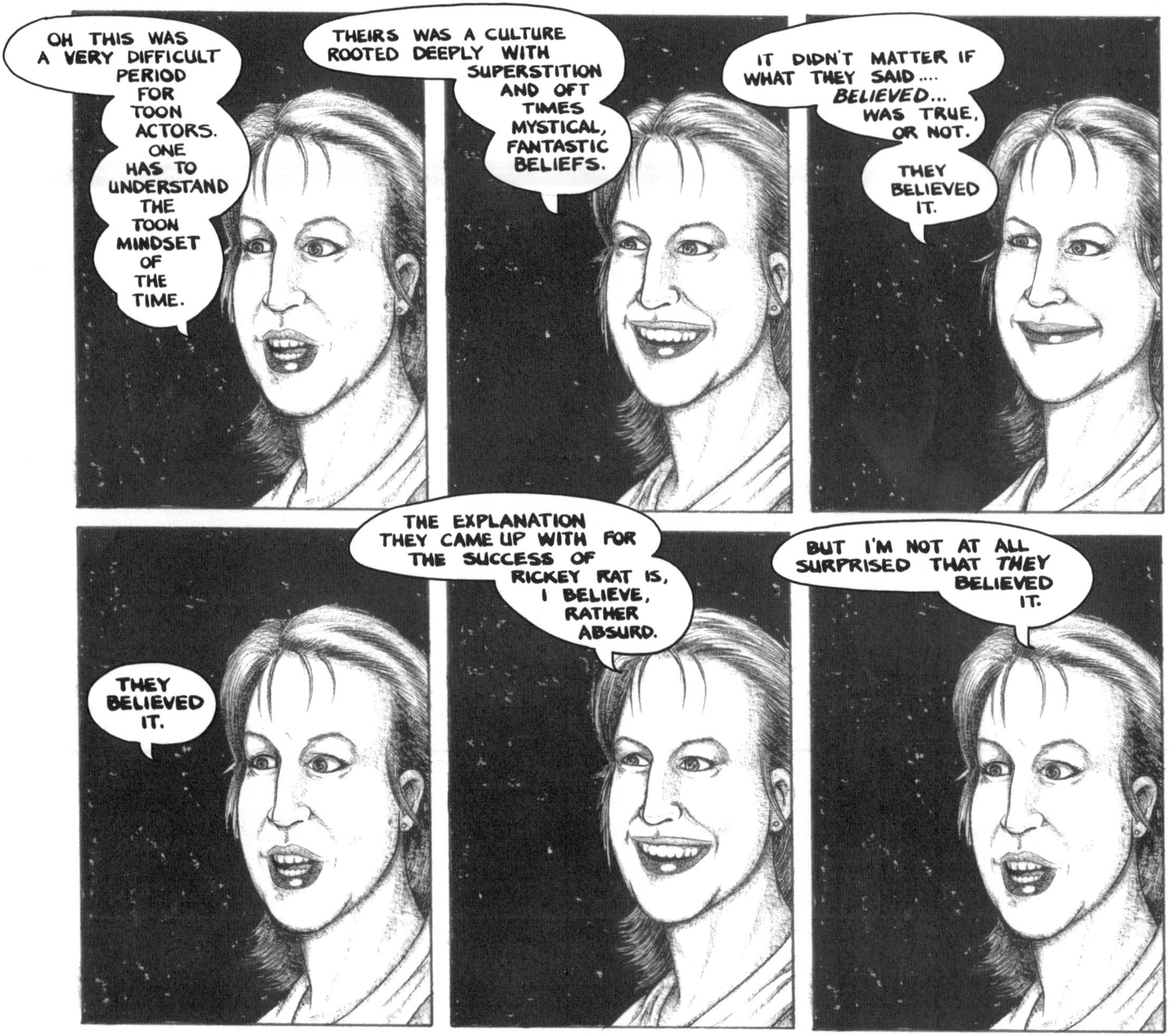
OH THIS WAS A VERY DIFFICULT PERIOD FOR TOON ACTORS. ONE HAS TO UNDERSTAND THE TOON MINDSET OF THE TIME.
THEIRS WAS A CULTURE ROOTED DEEPLY WITH SUPERSTITION AND OFT TIMES MYSTICAL, FANTASTIC BELIEFS.
IT DIDN'T MATTER IF WHAT THEY SAID.... *BELIEVED*... WAS TRUE, OR NOT.
THEY BELIEVED IT.
THEY BELIEVED IT.
THE EXPLANATION THEY CAME UP WITH FOR THE SUCCESS OF RICKEY RAT IS, I BELIEVE, RATHER ABSURD.
BUT I'M NOT AT ALL SURPRISED THAT *THEY* BELIEVED IT.

UM... WELL I... I... WELL...
HYACK!... HRMM!.. EXCUSE ME...
I... YES... I HEARD THE RUMORS....
OF THE... UH... THE UM... THE... THE...
THE RITUAL.

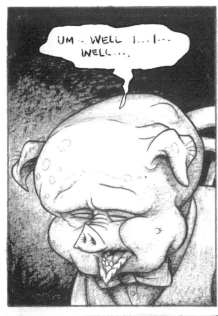

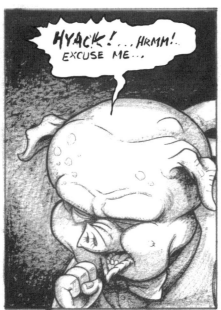

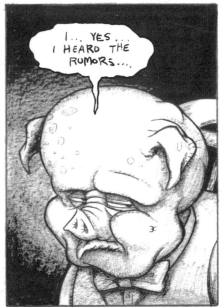

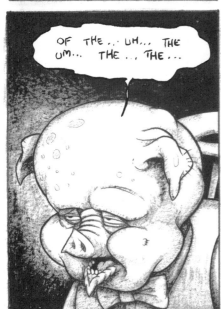

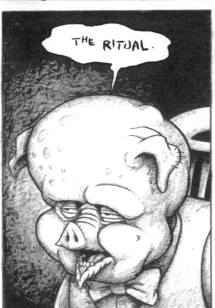

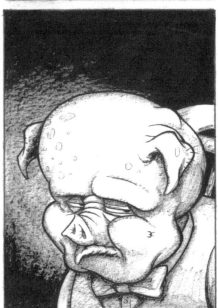

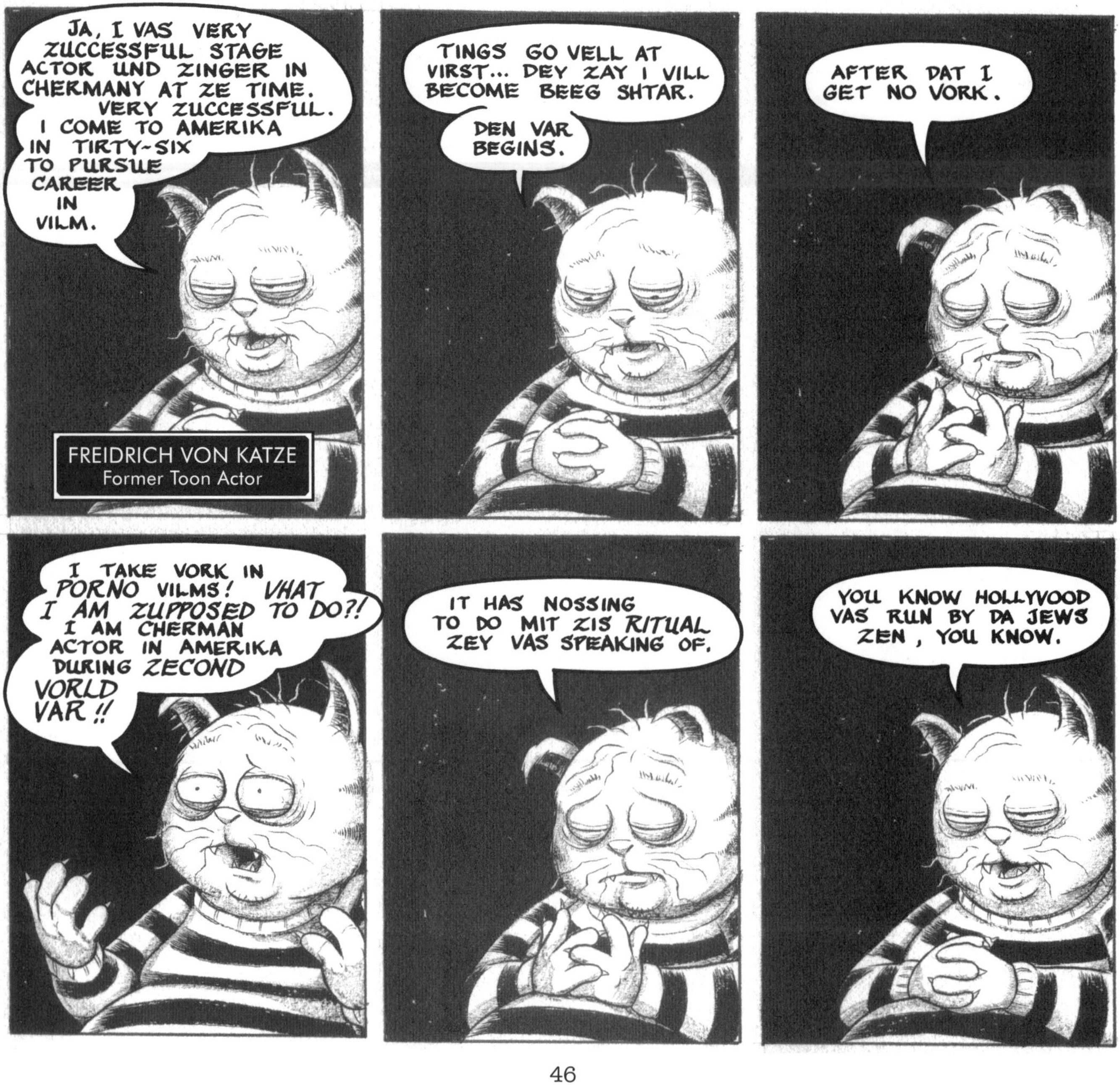

JA, I VAS VERY ZUCCESSFUL STAGE ACTOR UND ZINGER IN CHERMANY AT ZE TIME. VERY ZUCCESSFUL. I COME TO AMERIKA IN TIRTY-SIX TO PURSUE CAREER IN VILM.
FREIDRICH VON KATZE
Former Toon Actor
TINGS GO VELL AT VIRST... DEY ZAY I VILL BECOME BEEG SHTAR.
DEN VAR BEGINS.
AFTER DAT I GET NO VORK.
I TAKE VORK IN PORNO VILMS! VHAT I AM ZUPPOSED TO DO?! I AM CHERMAN ACTOR IN AMERIKA DURING ZECOND VORLD VAR!!
IT HAS NOSSING TO DO MIT ZIS RITUAL ZEY VAS SPEAKING OF.
YOU KNOW HOLLYVOOD VAS RUN BY DA JEWS ZEN, YOU KNOW.

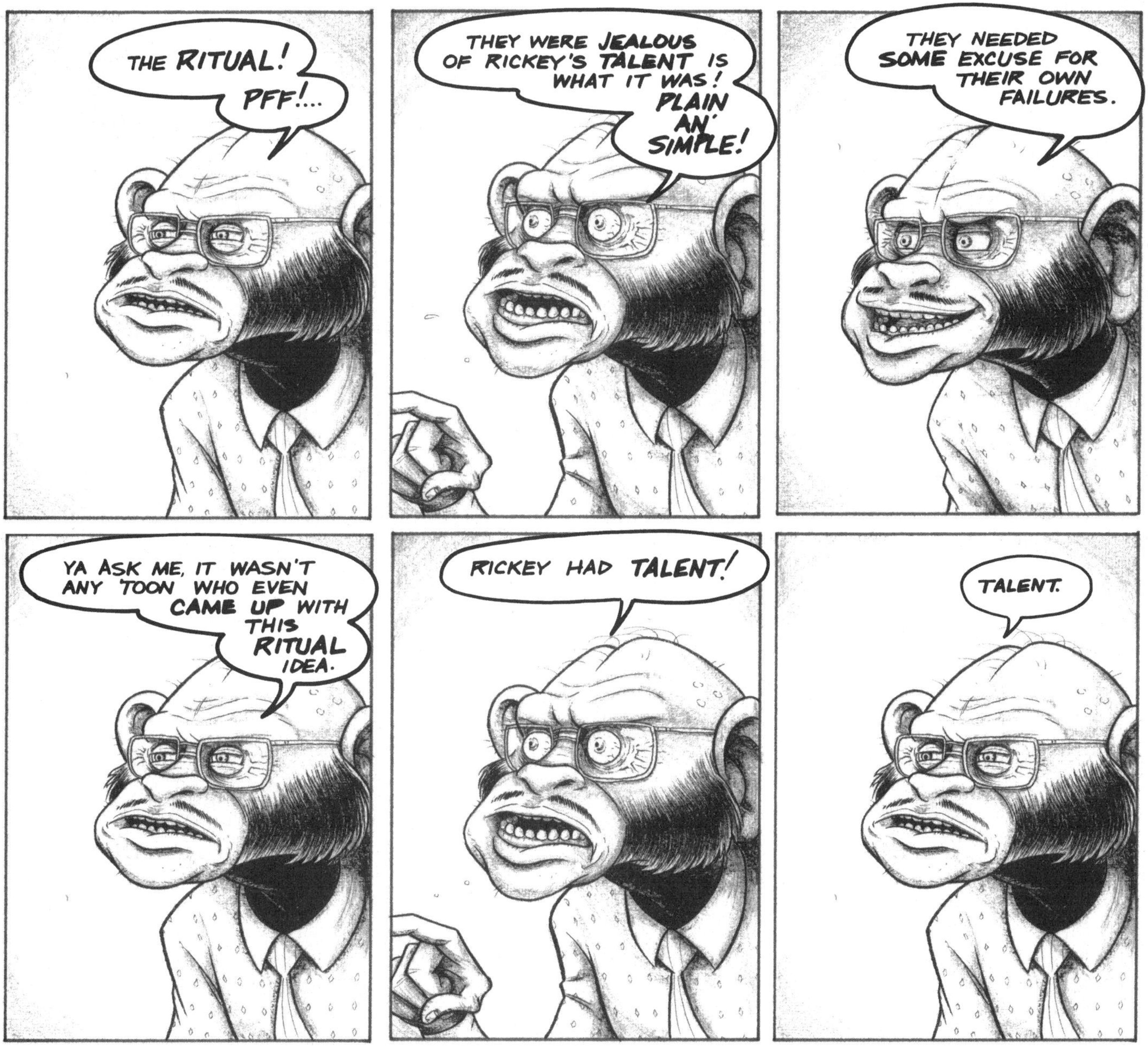
THE RITUAL!
PFF!...
THEY WERE JEALOUS OF RICKEY'S TALENT IS WHAT IT WAS!
PLAIN AN' SIMPLE!
THEY NEEDED SOME EXCUSE FOR THEIR OWN FAILURES.
YA ASK ME, IT WASN'T ANY 'TOON WHO EVEN CAME UP WITH THIS RITUAL IDEA.
RICKEY HAD TALENT!
TALENT.

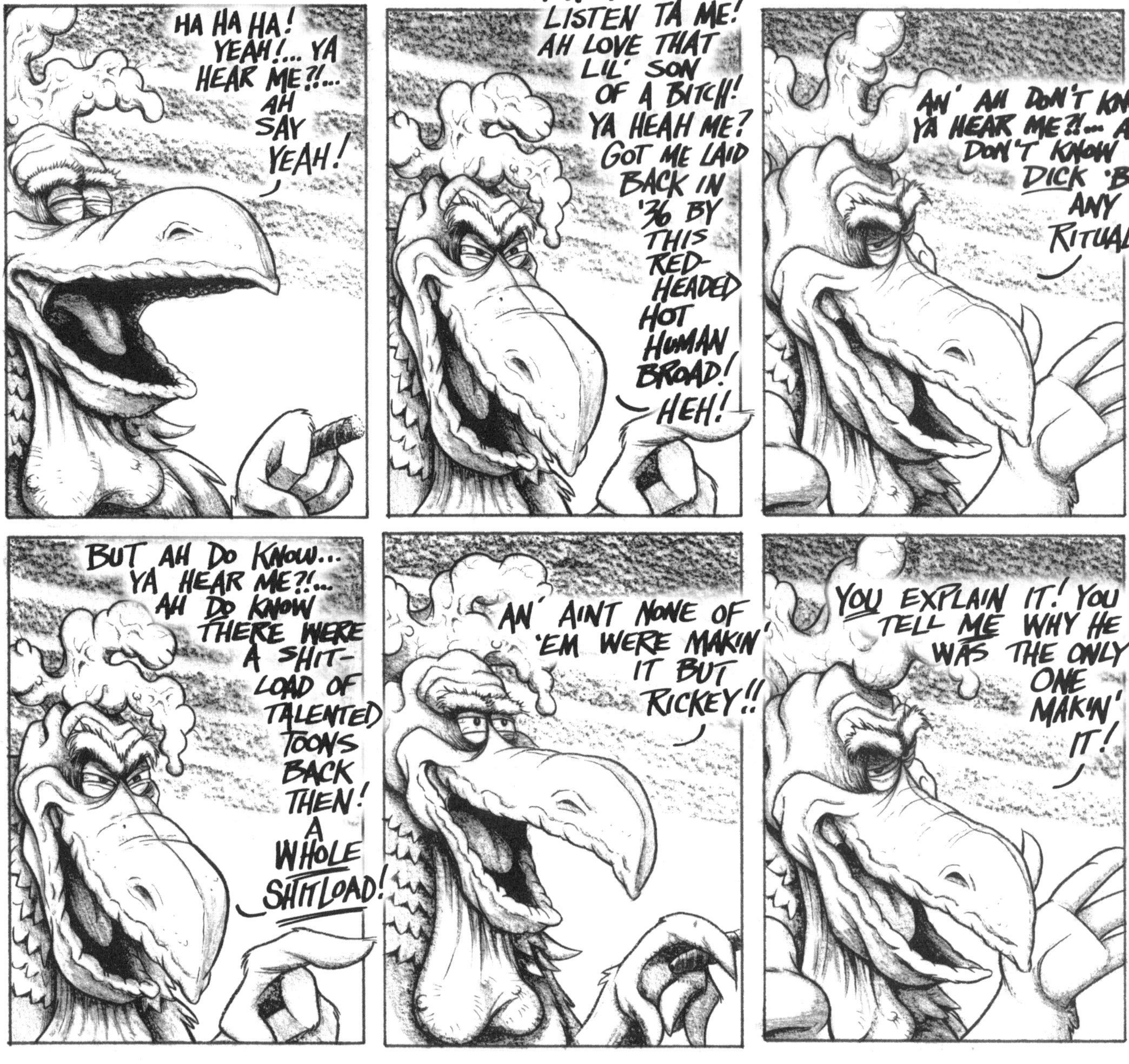
HA HA HA! YEAH!... YA HEAR ME?!... AH SAY YEAH!
NOW YOU LISTEN TA ME! AH LOVE THAT LIL' SON OF A BITCH! YA HEAH ME? GOT ME LAID BACK IN '36 BY THIS RED-HEADED HOT HUMAN BROAD! HEH!
AN' AH DON'T KNOW... YA HEAR ME?!... AH DON'T KNOW DICK 'BOUT ANY RITUAL!
BUT AH DO KNOW... YA HEAR ME?!... AH DO KNOW THERE WERE A SHIT-LOAD OF TALENTED TOONS BACK THEN! A WHOLE SHITLOAD!
AN' AINT NONE OF 'EM WERE MAKIN' IT BUT RICKEY!!
YOU EXPLAIN IT! YOU TELL ME WHY HE WAS THE ONLY ONE MAKIN' IT!

THE RITUAL

By 1946, Dizzy Walters and Rickey Rat had produced twelve feature-length cartoons, and some two dozen "shorts" together.

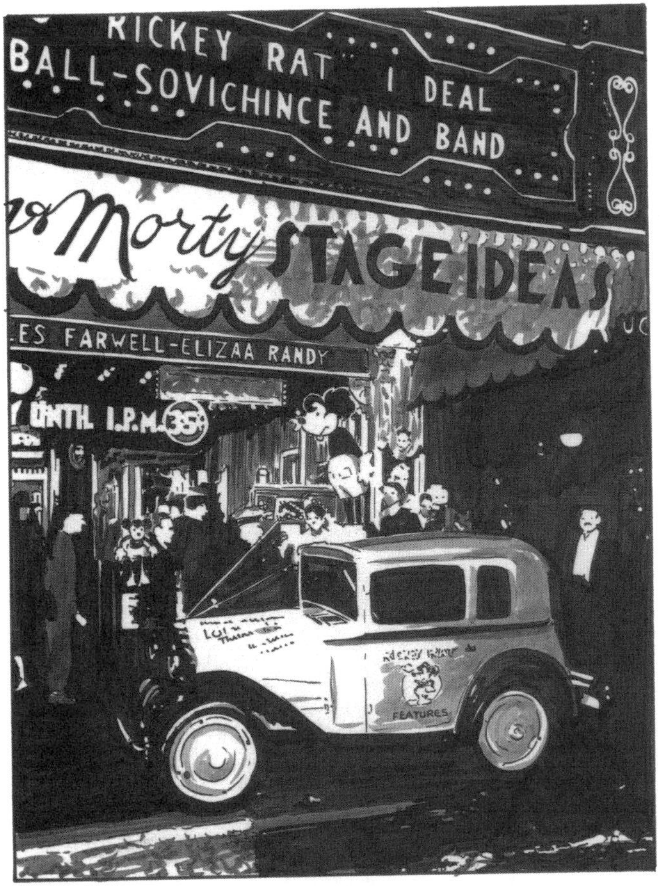
RICKEY RAT
I DEAL
BALL-SOVICHINCE AND BAND
Morty STAGE IDEAS
ES FARWELL-ELIZAA RANDY
FEATURES

And while hundreds of other cartoons were produced, and dozens of other talented Toons surfaced during the two decades that Dizzy and Rickey were together, only THEIR films prospered, and only Rickey emerged as a bonafide Toon Superstar.

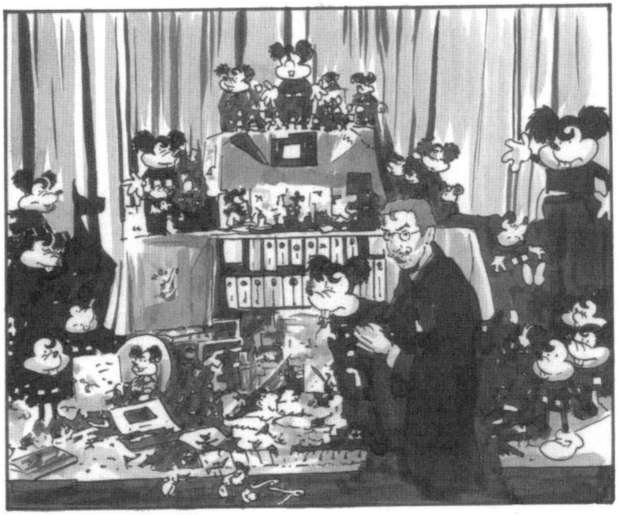

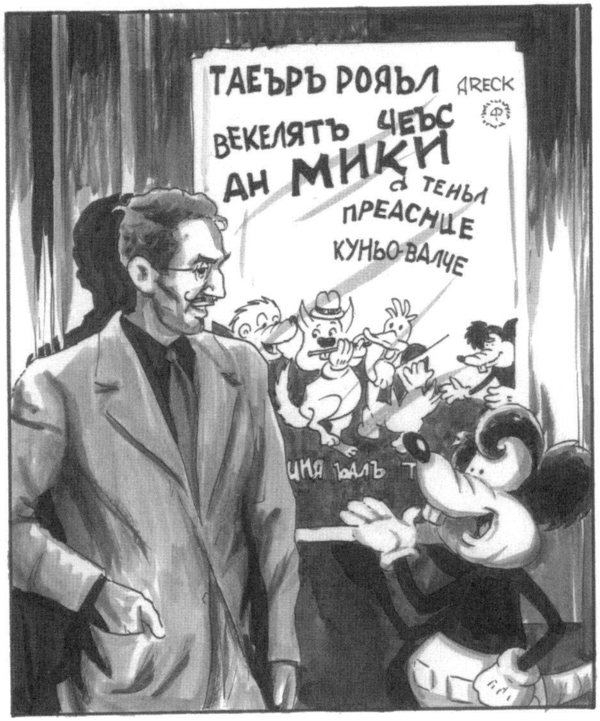
ТАЕЪРЪ РОЯЬЛ
ARECK
ВЕКЕЛЯТЪ ЧЕЪС
ДН МИКИ
а ТЕНЬЛ
ПРЕАСНЦЕ
КУНЬО-ВАЛЧЕ

Rickey Rat was married, briefly, to a young Toon bar waitress years before he met Dizzy Walters and became the world-famous Toon Superstar he now found himself to be. It was passionate, impulsive, and very brief. The divorce was amicable, and uneventful.

Rickey's second wife, an alluring New York stage actress and singer named ROSA BELMONT-- a HUMAN actress-- would prove to be the source of much more controversy. Rickey and Rosa were breaking barriers, and what most felt, taboos, that both enraged and delighted the American public.

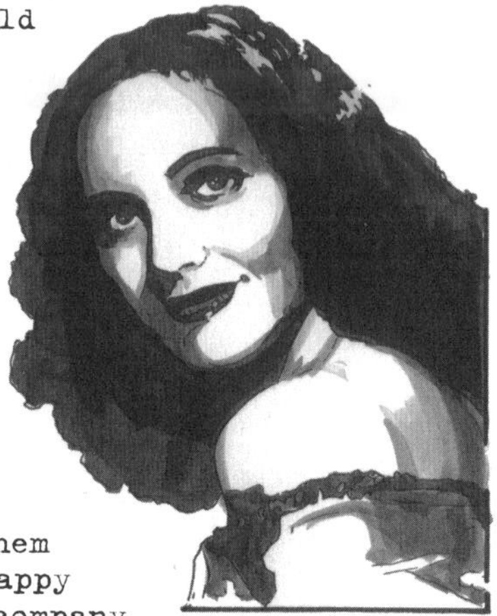

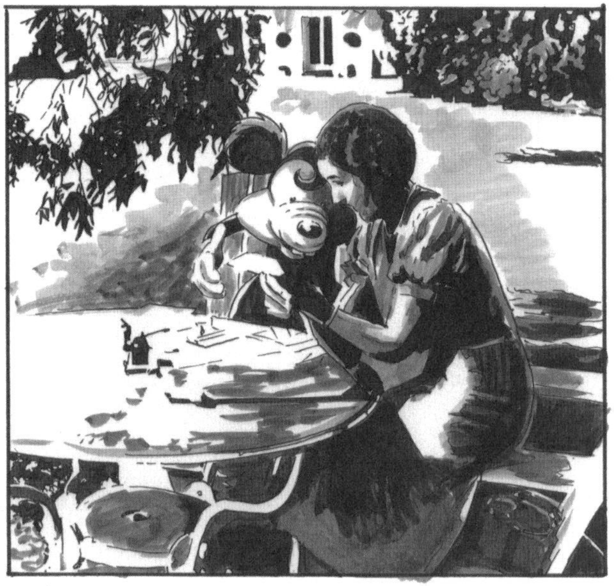

Close friends would insist the marriage was "true love." That the two of them were never more happy than when in the company of one another.

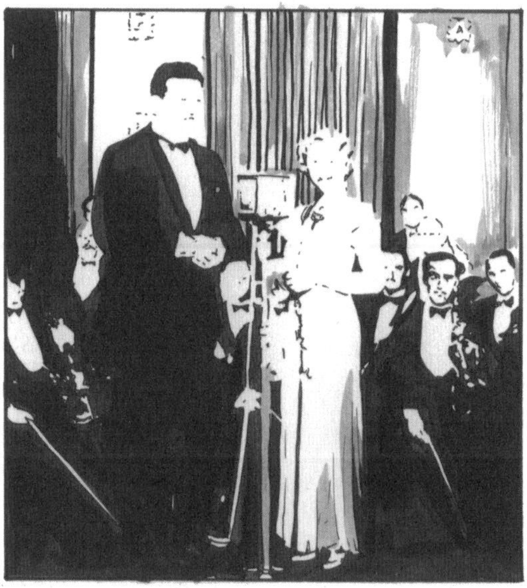

Some felt the marriage was merely a publicity stunt aimed at deflecting the rumors now surfacing about Rickey's success.

Whatever the reasons for the marriage, the strain of the public scrutiny and the whisperings of "The Ritual" were beginning to show on Rickey. He was beginning to drink, and close sources suggest his indulgences went beyond the bottle.

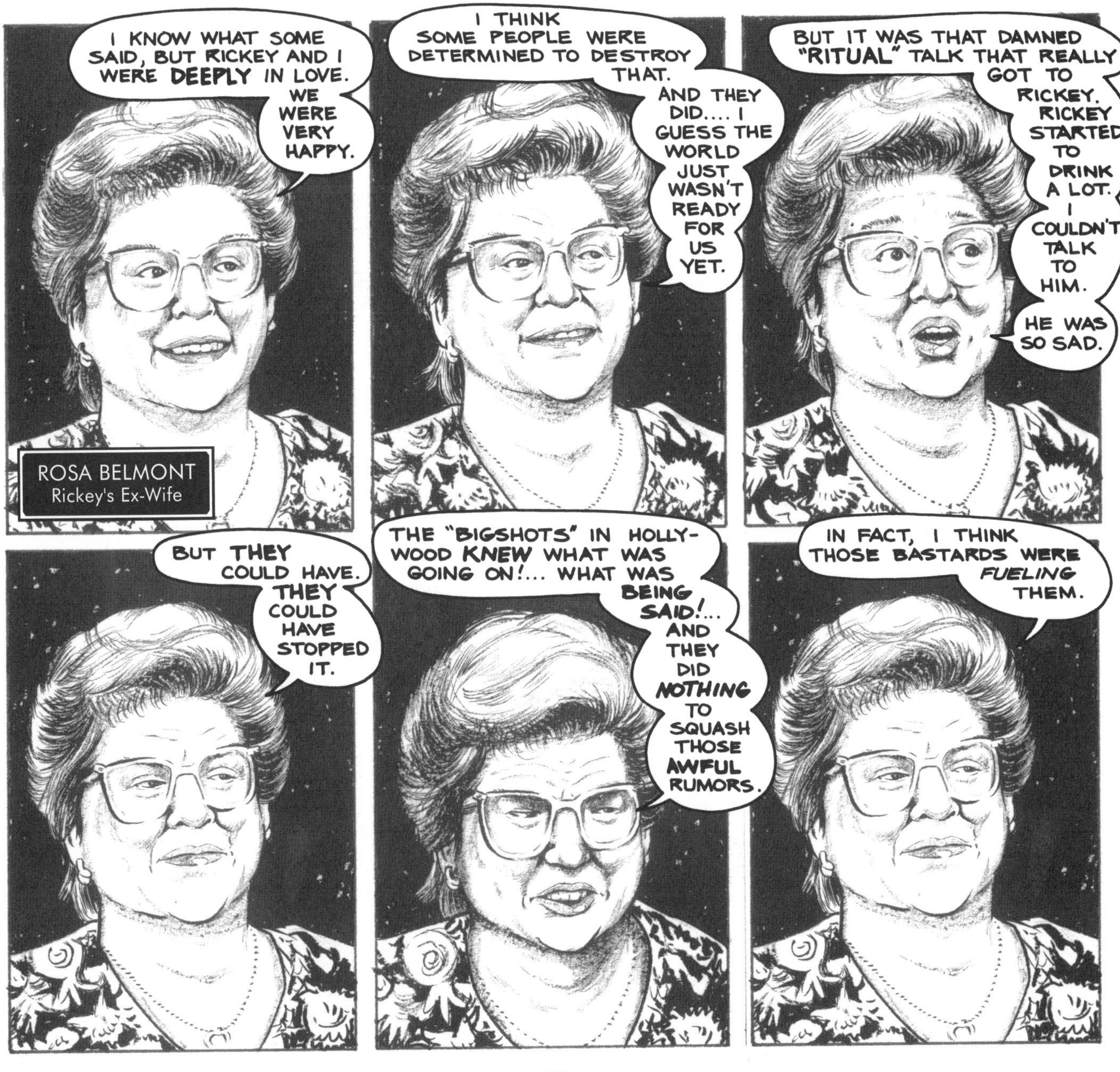
I KNOW WHAT SOME SAID, BUT RICKEY AND I WERE **DEEPLY** IN LOVE.
WE WERE VERY HAPPY.
ROSA BELMONT
Rickey's Ex-Wife
I THINK SOME PEOPLE WERE DETERMINED TO DESTROY THAT.
AND THEY DID.... I GUESS THE WORLD JUST WASN'T READY FOR US YET.
BUT IT WAS THAT DAMNED **"RITUAL"** TALK THAT REALLY GOT TO RICKEY.
RICKEY STARTED TO DRINK A LOT. I COULDN'T TALK TO HIM.
HE WAS SO SAD.
BUT **THEY** COULD HAVE.
THEY COULD HAVE STOPPED IT.
THE "BIGSHOTS" IN HOLLYWOOD **KNEW** WHAT WAS GOING ON!... WHAT WAS **BEING SAID**!...
AND THEY DID ***NOTHING*** TO SQUASH THOSE **AWFUL** RUMORS.
IN FACT, I THINK THOSE BASTARDS WERE *FUELING* THEM.

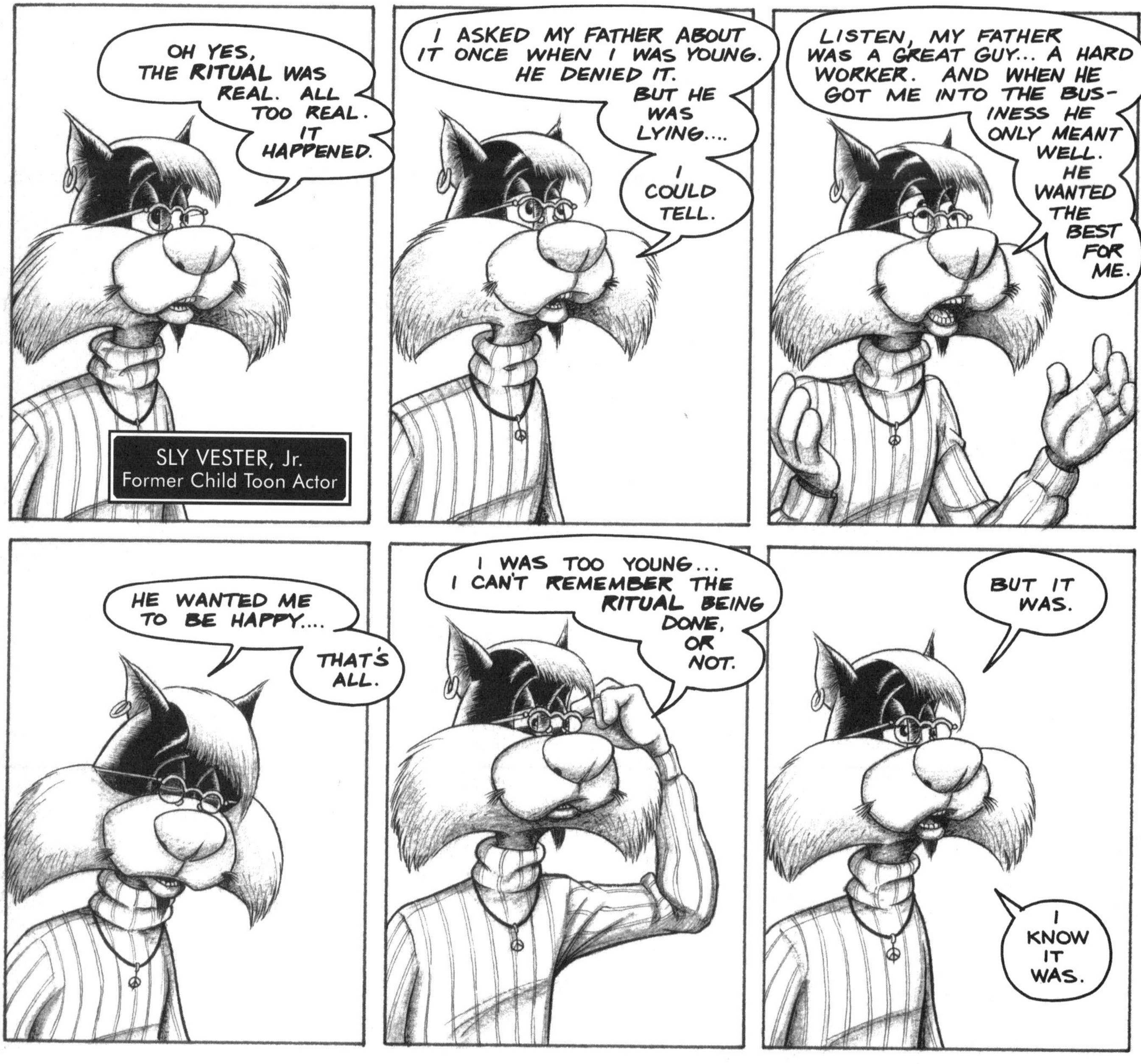
OH YES, THE RITUAL WAS REAL. ALL TOO REAL. IT HAPPENED.
SLY VESTER, Jr.
Former Child Toon Actor
I ASKED MY FATHER ABOUT IT ONCE WHEN I WAS YOUNG. HE DENIED IT.
BUT HE WAS LYING....
I COULD TELL.
LISTEN, MY FATHER WAS A GREAT GUY... A HARD WORKER. AND WHEN HE GOT ME INTO THE BUS-INESS HE ONLY MEANT WELL.
HE WANTED THE BEST FOR ME.
HE WANTED ME TO BE HAPPY....
THAT'S ALL.
I WAS TOO YOUNG... I CAN'T REMEMBER THE RITUAL BEING DONE, OR NOT.
BUT IT WAS.
I KNOW IT WAS.

EVERYTHING WAS GOING FINE....
JUST FINE.
UNTIL THOSE DAMNED PICTURES SURFACED.

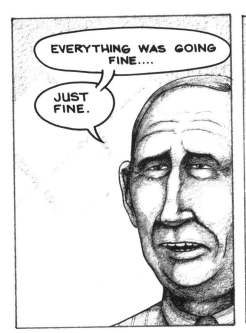

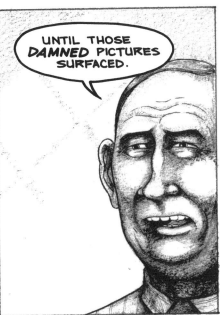

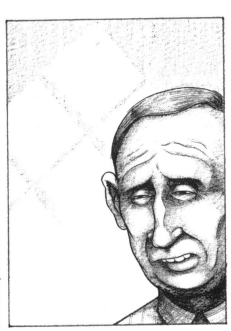

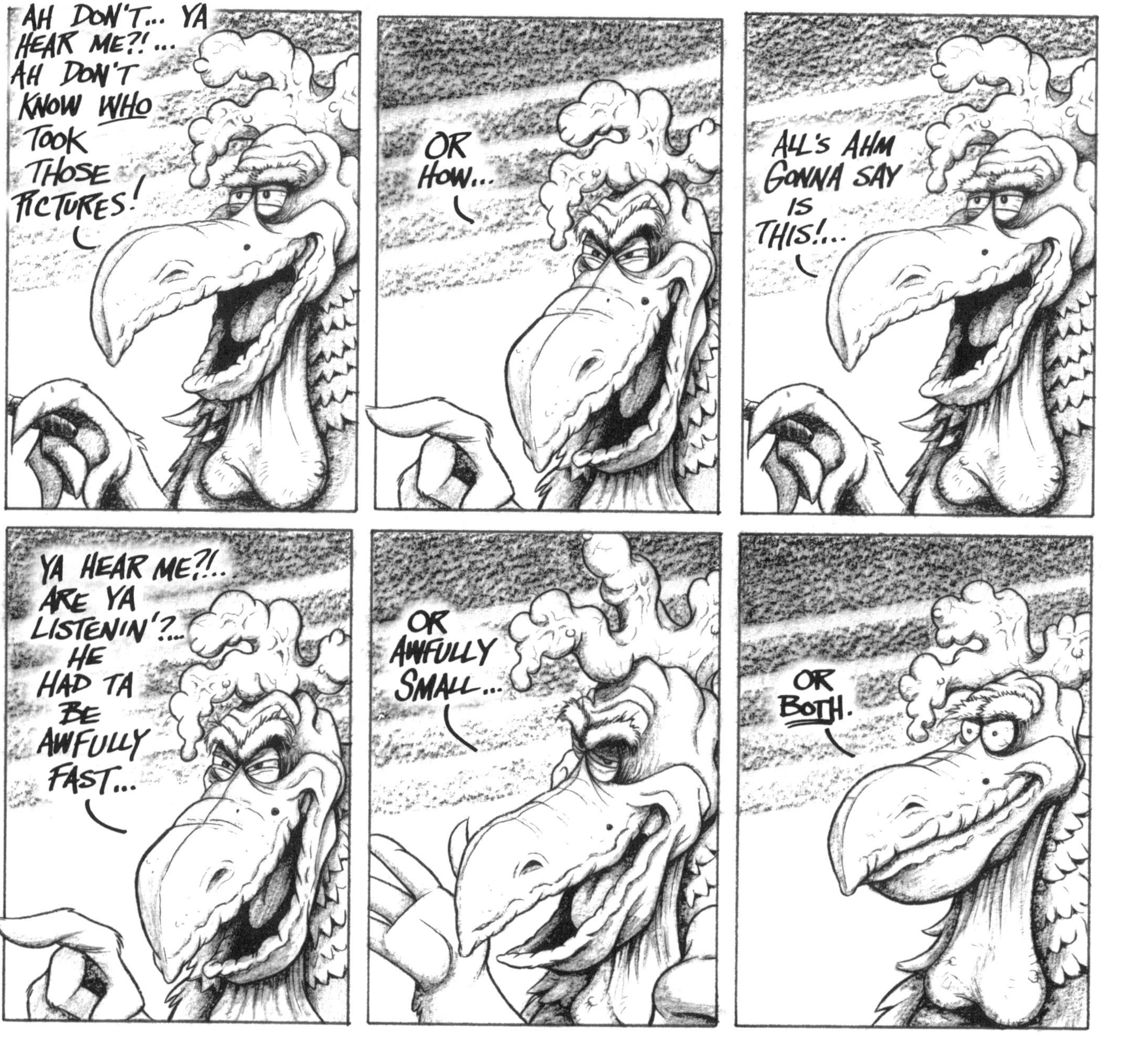
AH DON'T... YA HEAR ME?!... AH DON'T KNOW WHO TOOK THOSE PICTURES!
OR HOW...
ALL'S AHM GONNA SAY IS THIS!...
YA HEAR ME?!... ARE YA LISTENIN'?... HE HAD TA BE AWFULLY FAST...
OR AWFULLY SMALL...
OR BOTH.

In 1948, at the height of Dizzy Walters' and Rickey Rat's popularity, and also at the height of the rumors surrounding "The Ritual," a series of mysterious photographs would surface; further fueling speculation that the rumored Ritual was, in fact, a HORRIBLE REALITY.

The photos, although of poor quality,
clearly show a surgical procedure of
some kind taking place.

The poor quality of the photos would suggest the photographer
was taking them rather quickly, and was most likely taking them
without the consent of the subjects in the photos.

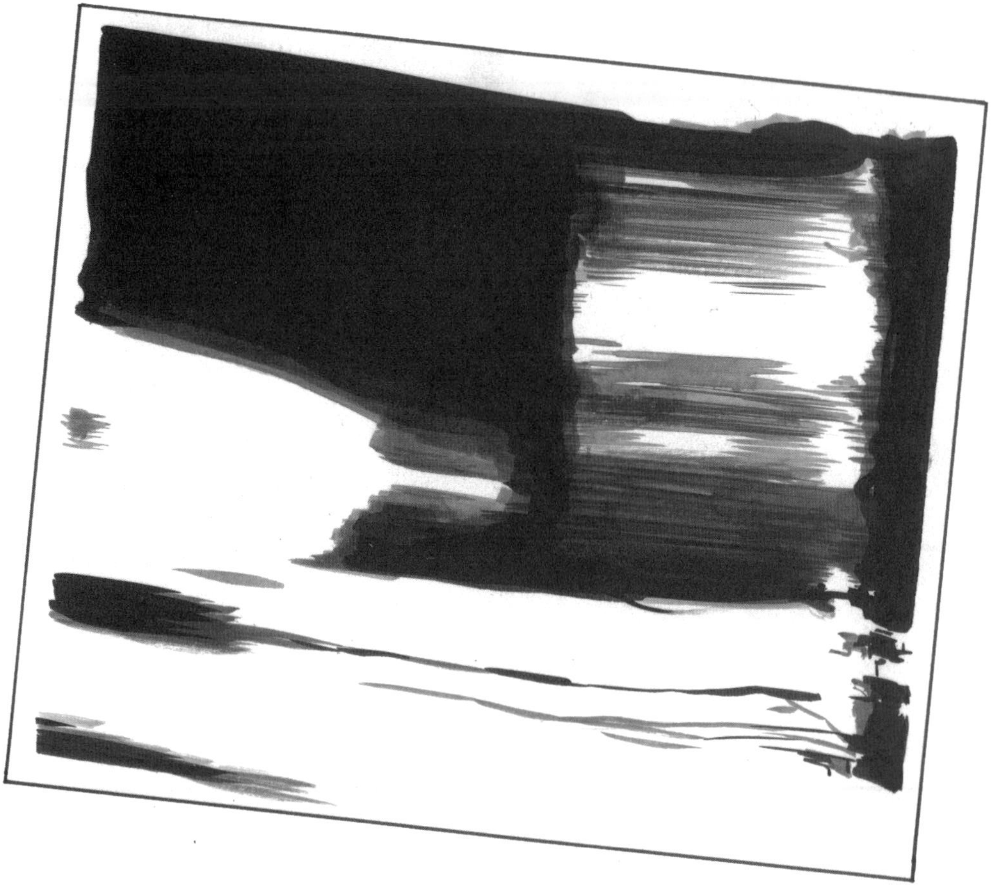

The origin of the photographs, and the identity of the photographer, were, and to this day still remain, the subject of much discussion and debate.

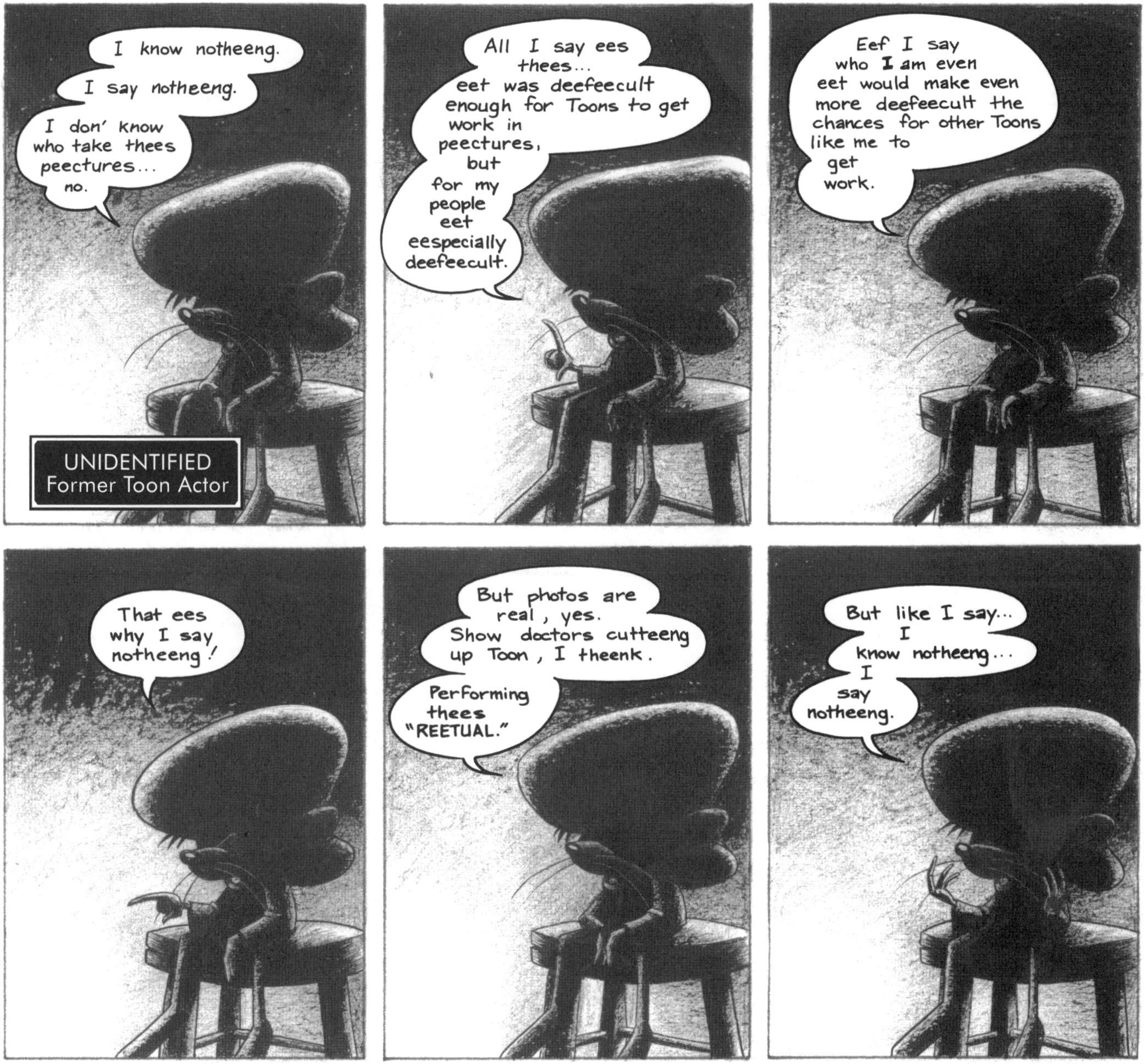
I know notheeng.
I say notheeng.
I don' know who take thees peectures... no.
UNIDENTIFIED Former Toon Actor
All I say ees thees... eet was deefeecult enough for Toons to get work in peectures, but for my people eet eespecially deefeecult.
Eef I say who I am even eet would make even more deefeecult the chances for other Toons like me to get work.
That ees why I say notheeng!
But photos are real, yes. Show doctors cutteeng up Toon, I theenk.
Performing thees "REETUAL."
But like I say... I know notheeng...
I say notheeng.

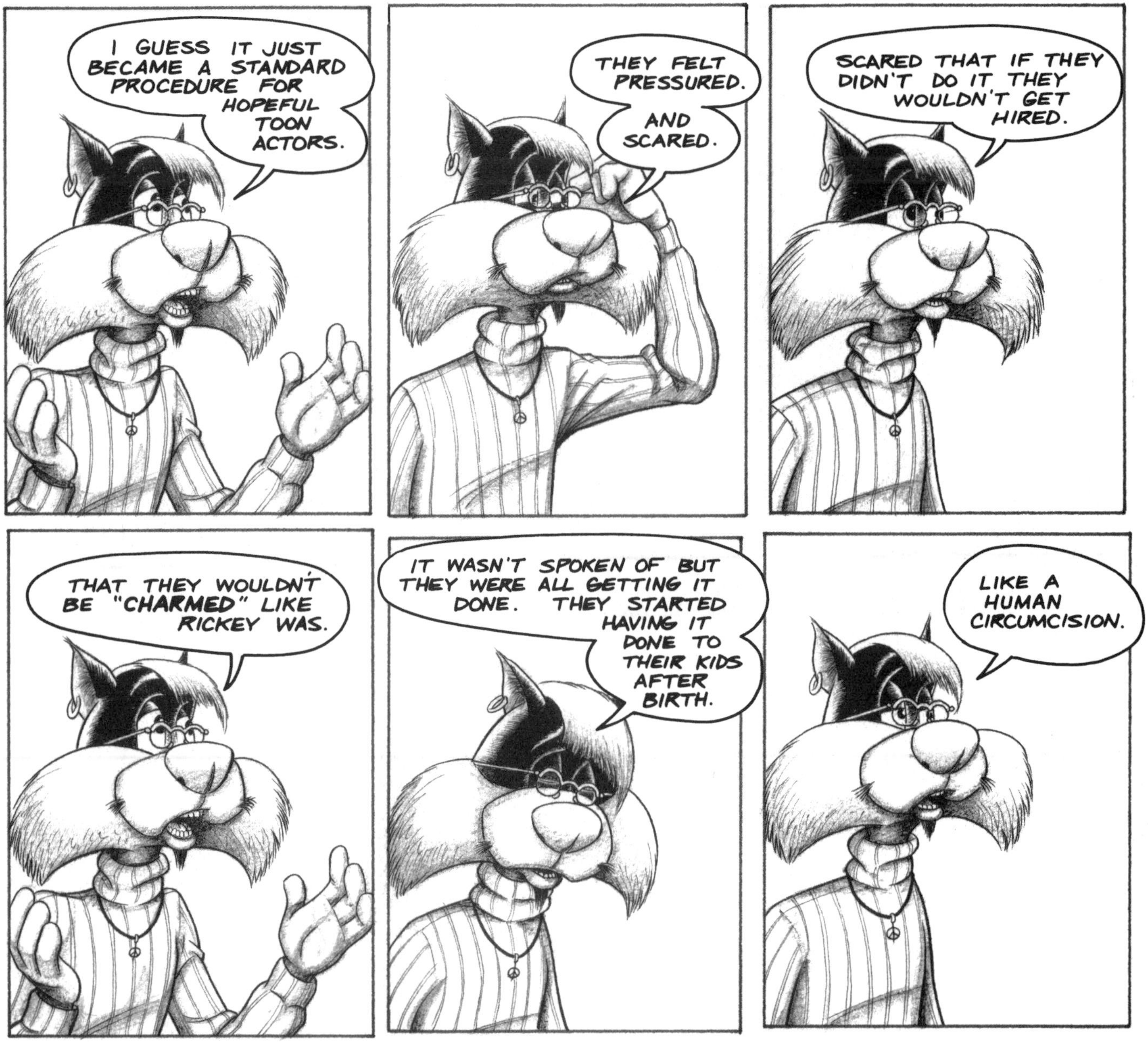
I GUESS IT JUST BECAME A STANDARD PROCEDURE FOR HOPEFUL TOON ACTORS.
THEY FELT PRESSURED.
AND SCARED.
SCARED THAT IF THEY DIDN'T DO IT THEY WOULDN'T GET HIRED.
THAT THEY WOULDN'T BE "CHARMED" LIKE RICKEY WAS.
IT WASN'T SPOKEN OF BUT THEY WERE ALL GETTING IT DONE. THEY STARTED HAVING IT DONE TO THEIR KIDS AFTER BIRTH.
LIKE A HUMAN CIRCUMCISION.

THEY WERE CUTTING OFF THEIR FINGERS!..
TO BE LIKE ME....
MY GOD!... THEIR FINGERS!

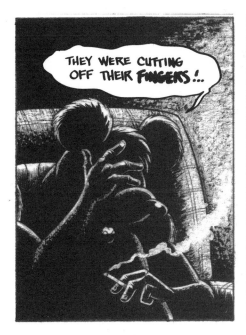

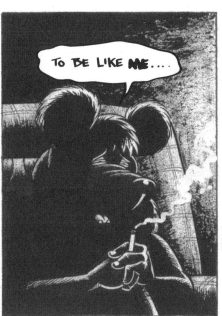

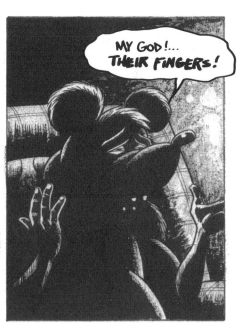

It seems that frustrated
Toon actors became convinced
that Rickey Rat's "Star Power"
was related to the fact that he
was born with only three fingers.
That because of his birth defect,
he was somehow "charmed."

So hopeful Toon actors began
to have their fourth fingers removed,
in hopes that their luck would change.

As the decade of the 1940s neared its end, a rash of new Toon superstars emerged.

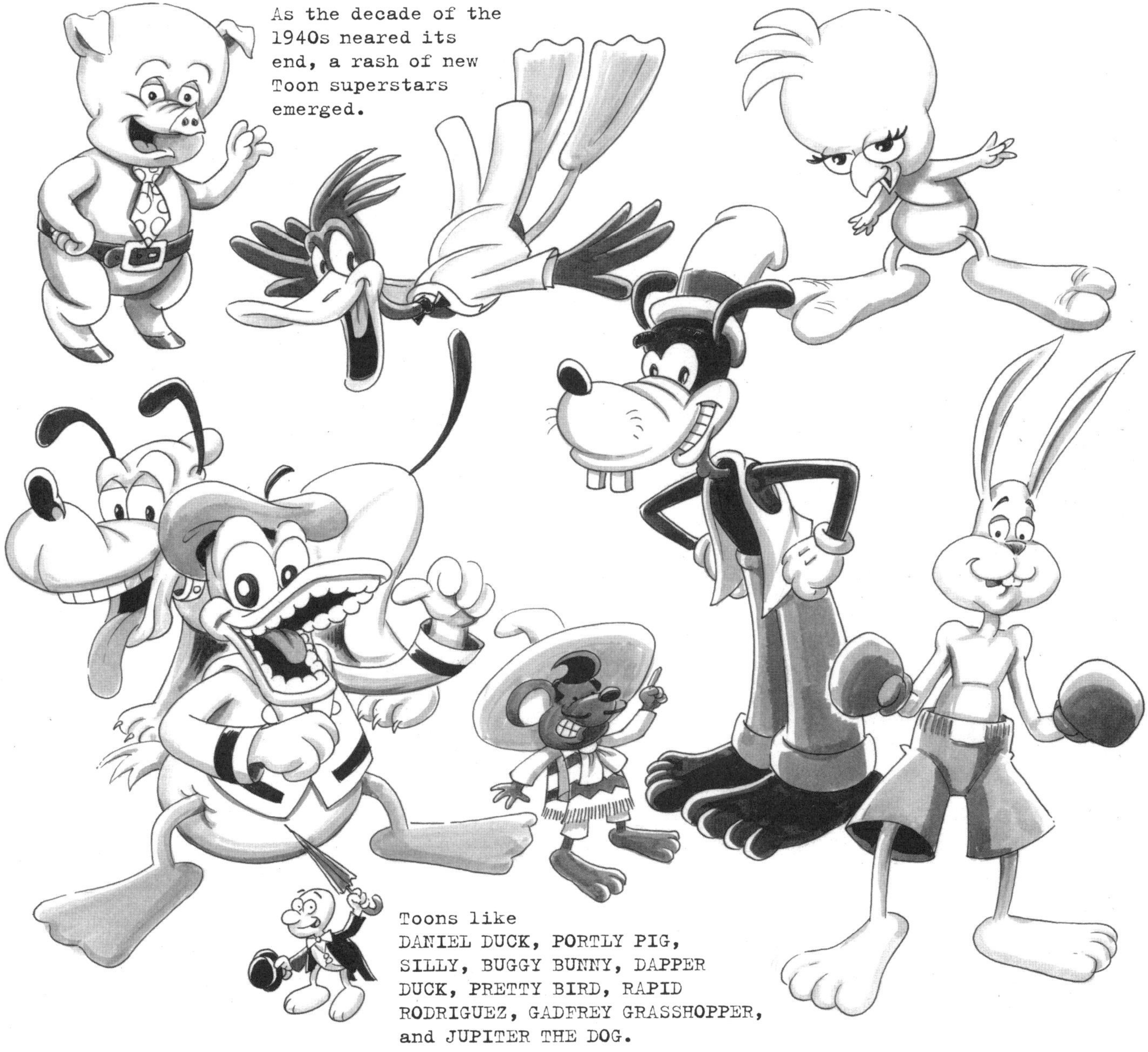

Toons like DANIEL DUCK, PORTLY PIG, SILLY, BUGGY BUNNY, DAPPER DUCK, PRETTY BIRD, RAPID RODRIGUEZ, GADFREY GRASSHOPPER, and JUPITER THE DOG.

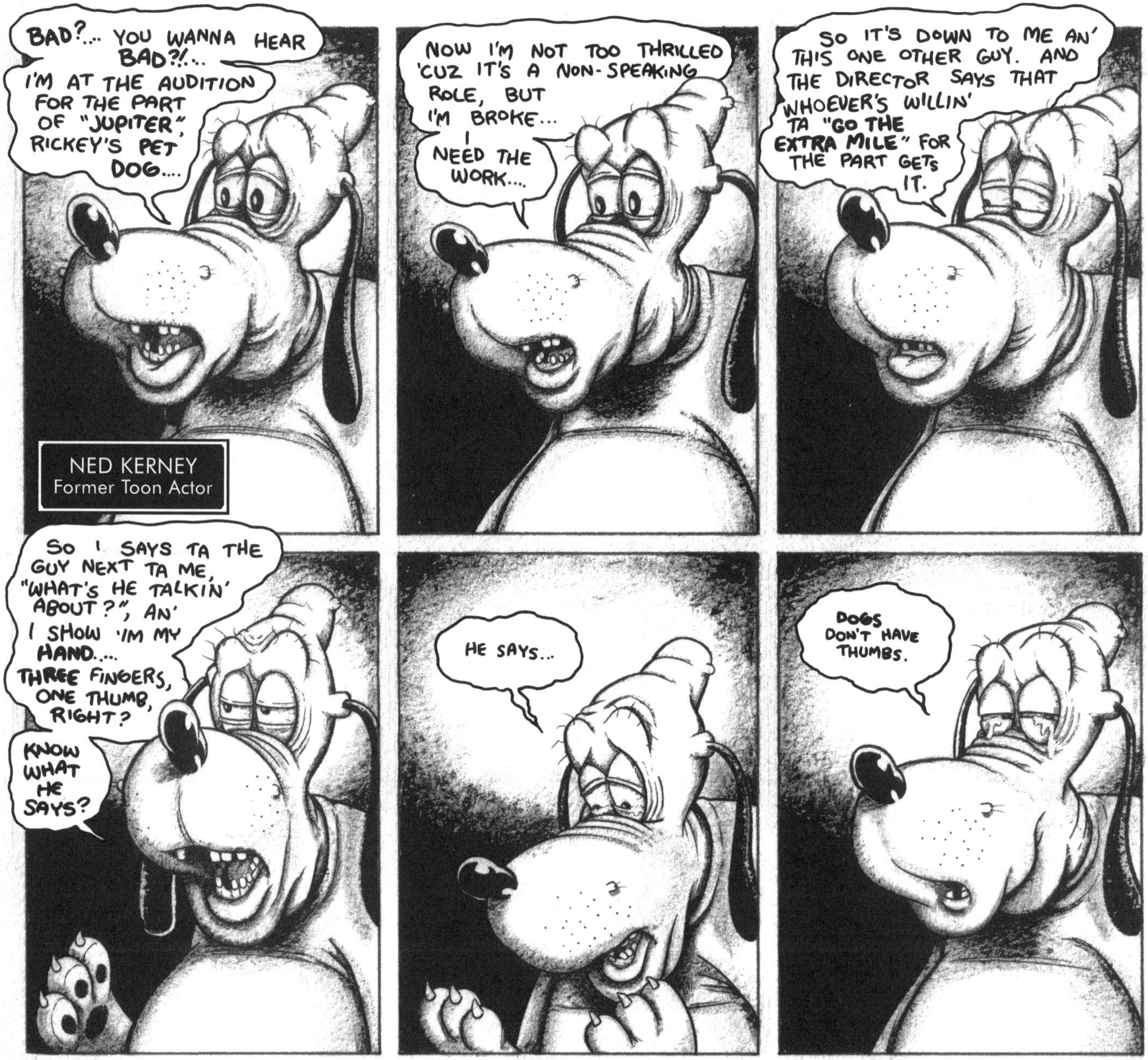
BAD?... YOU WANNA HEAR BAD?!...
I'M AT THE AUDITION FOR THE PART OF "JUPITER", RICKEY'S PET DOG....
NED KERNEY
Former Toon Actor
NOW I'M NOT TOO THRILLED 'CUZ IT'S A NON-SPEAKING ROLE, BUT I'M BROKE...
I NEED THE WORK....
SO IT'S DOWN TO ME AN' THIS ONE OTHER GUY. AND THE DIRECTOR SAYS THAT WHOEVER'S WILLIN' TA "GO THE EXTRA MILE" FOR THE PART GETS IT.
SO I SAYS TA THE GUY NEXT TA ME, "WHAT'S HE TALKIN' ABOUT?", AN' I SHOW 'IM MY HAND.... THREE FINGERS, ONE THUMB, RIGHT?
KNOW WHAT HE SAYS?
HE SAYS...
DOGS DON'T HAVE THUMBS.

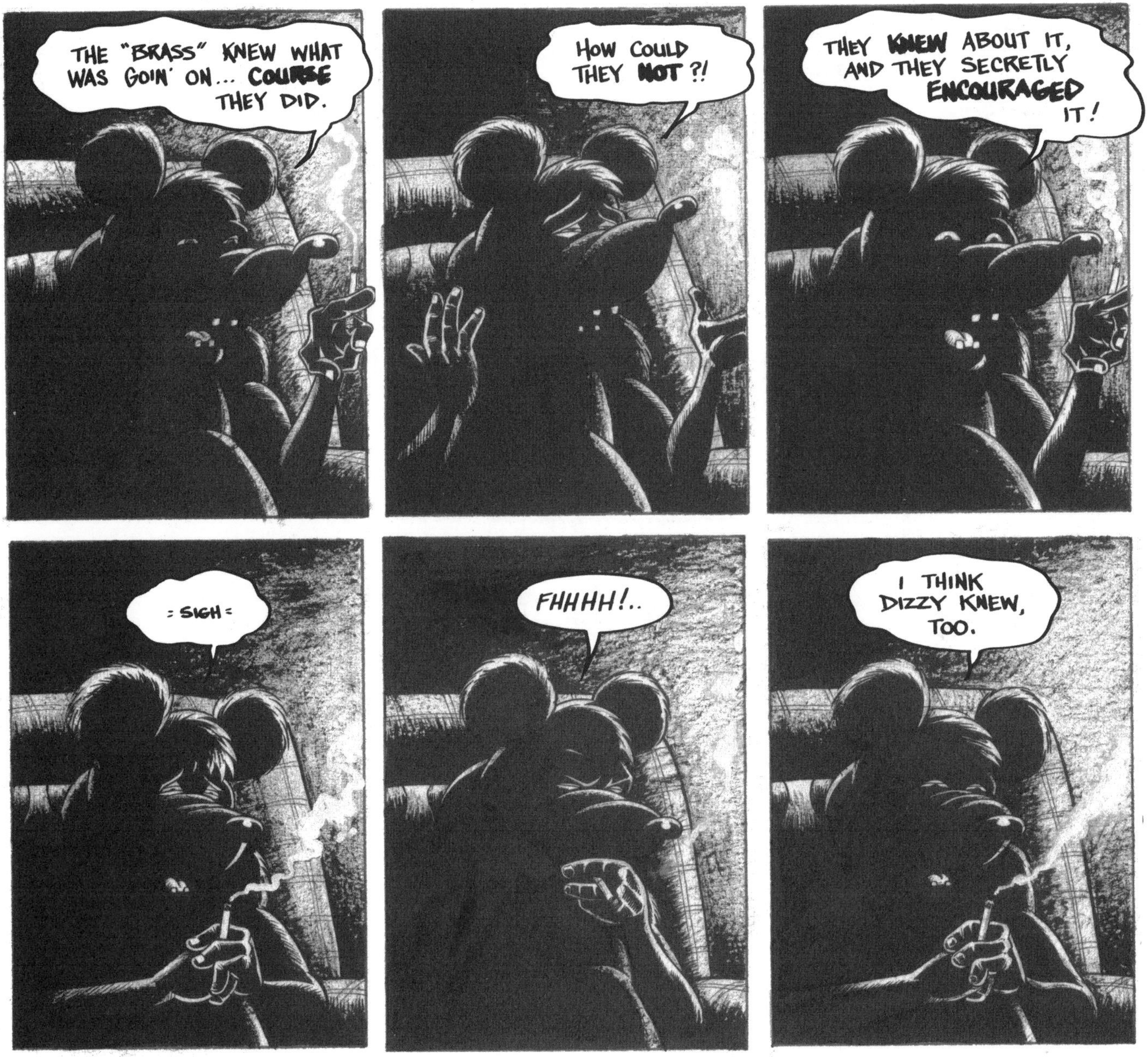
THE "BRASS" KNEW WHAT WAS GOIN' ON... COURSE THEY DID.
HOW COULD THEY NOT ?!
THEY KNEW ABOUT IT, AND THEY SECRETLY ENCOURAGED IT!
= SIGH =
FHHHH!..
I THINK DIZZY KNEW, TOO.

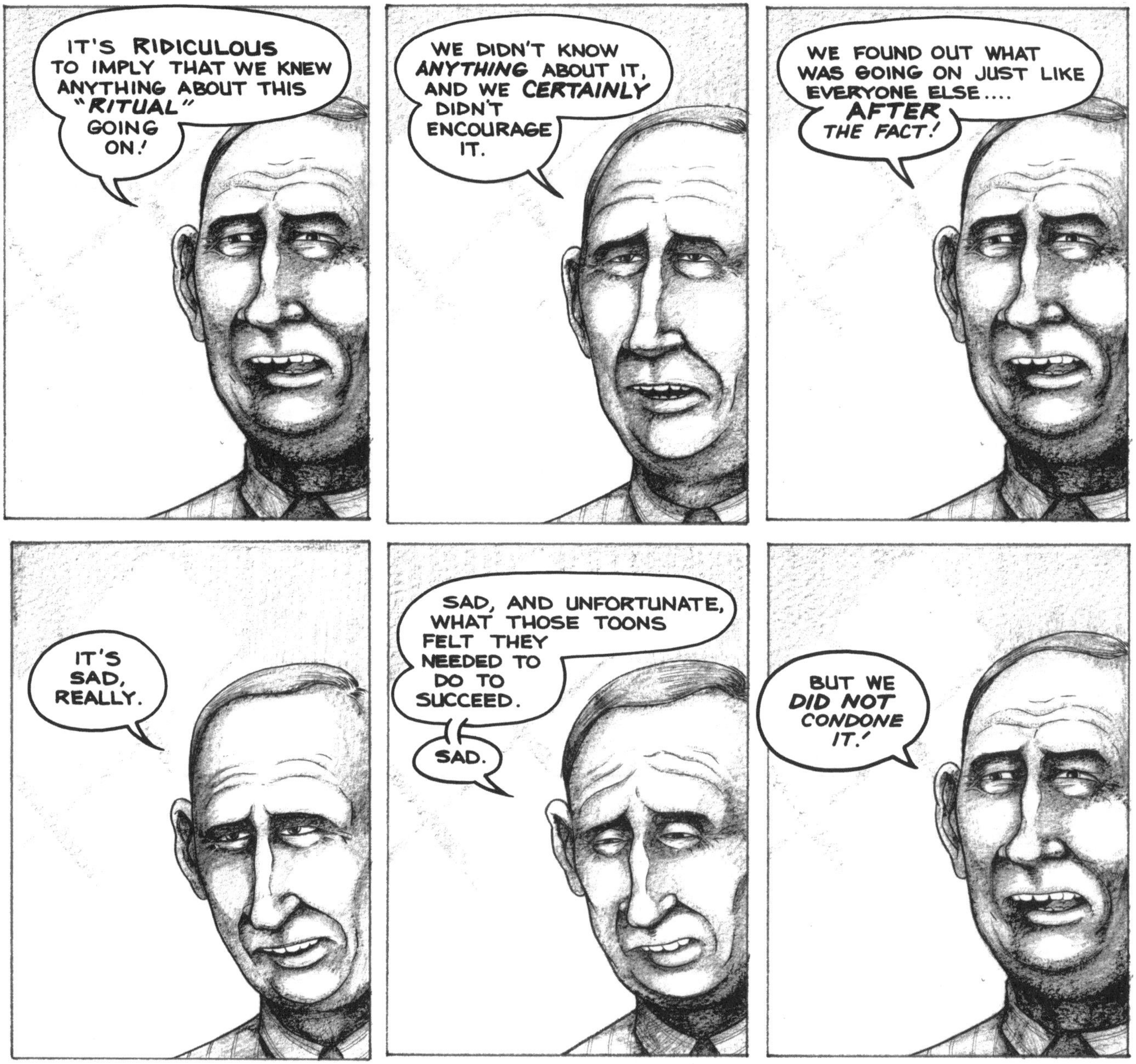
IT'S RIDICULOUS TO IMPLY THAT WE KNEW ANYTHING ABOUT THIS "RITUAL" GOING ON!
WE DIDN'T KNOW ANYTHING ABOUT IT, AND WE CERTAINLY DIDN'T ENCOURAGE IT.
WE FOUND OUT WHAT WAS GOING ON JUST LIKE EVERYONE ELSE.... AFTER THE FACT!
IT'S SAD, REALLY.
SAD, AND UNFORTUNATE, WHAT THOSE TOONS FELT THEY NEEDED TO DO TO SUCCEED.
SAD.
BUT WE DID NOT CONDONE IT!

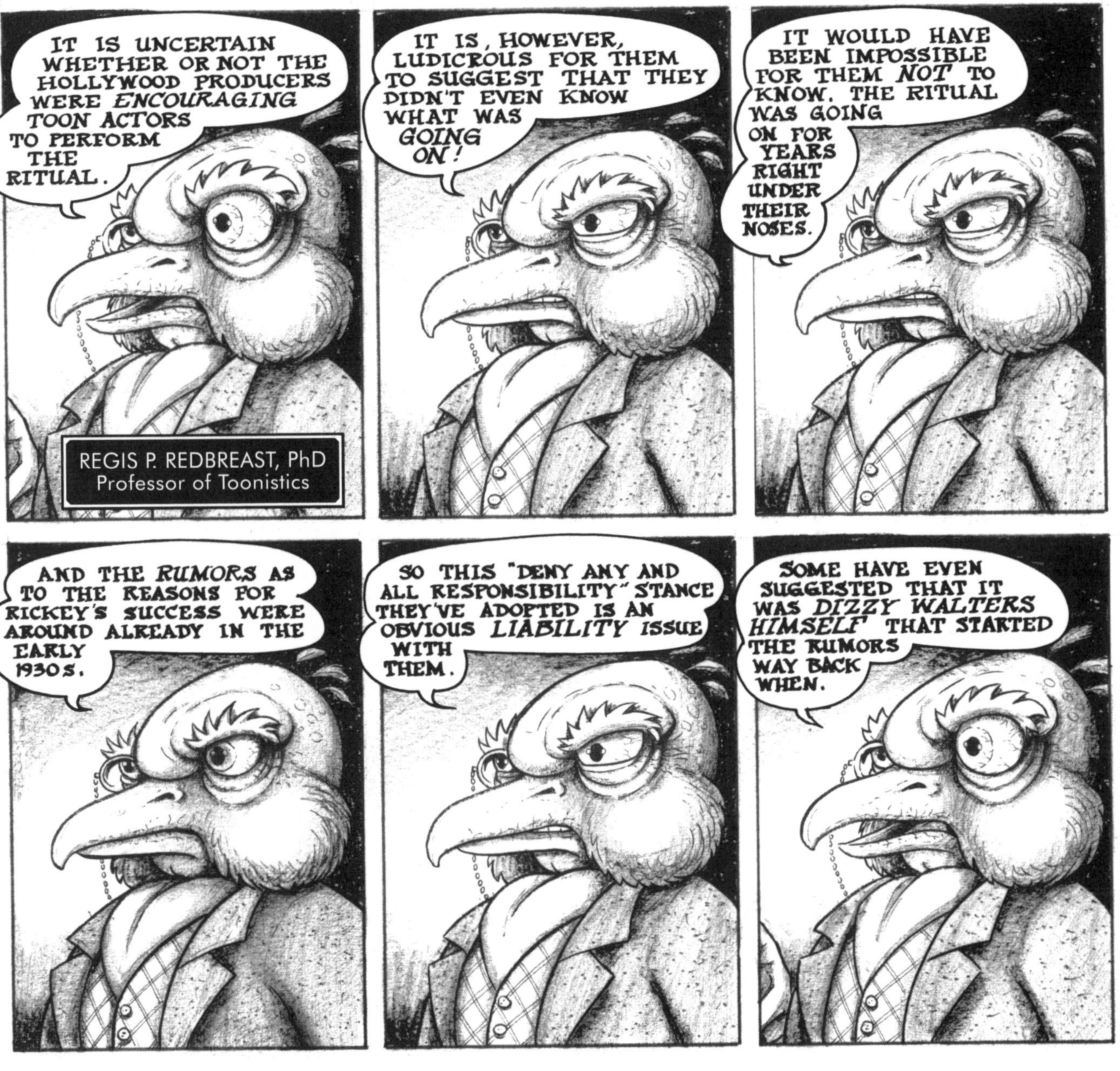
IT IS UNCERTAIN WHETHER OR NOT THE HOLLYWOOD PRODUCERS WERE *ENCOURAGING* TOON ACTORS TO PERFORM THE RITUAL.
REGIS P. REDBREAST, PhD
Professor of Toonistics
IT IS, HOWEVER, LUDICROUS FOR THEM TO SUGGEST THAT THEY DIDN'T EVEN KNOW WHAT WAS *GOING ON!*
IT WOULD HAVE BEEN IMPOSSIBLE FOR THEM *NOT* TO KNOW. THE RITUAL WAS GOING ON FOR YEARS RIGHT UNDER THEIR NOSES.
AND THE *RUMORS* AS TO THE REASONS FOR RICKEY'S SUCCESS WERE AROUND ALREADY IN THE EARLY 1930S.
SO THIS "DENY ANY AND ALL RESPONSIBILITY" STANCE THEY'VE ADOPTED IS AN OBVIOUS *LIABILITY* ISSUE WITH THEM.
SOME HAVE EVEN SUGGESTED THAT IT WAS *DIZZY WALTERS HIMSELF* THAT STARTED THE RUMORS WAY BACK WHEN.

A short time after the mysterious photographs surfaced, several secret "closed-door" meetings were held by Hollywood's biggest studios.

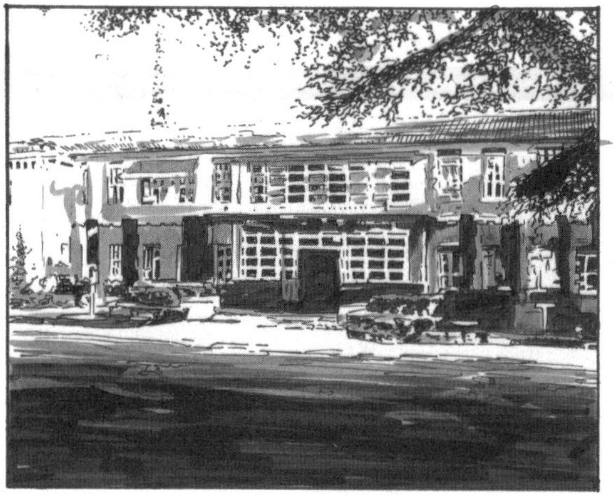

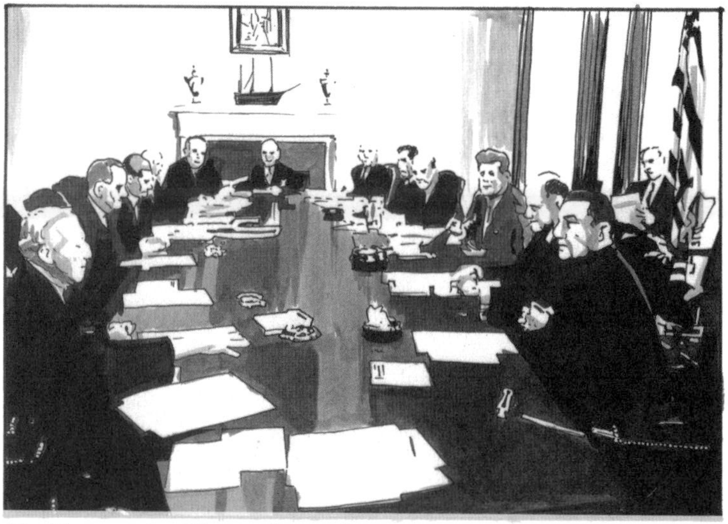

Whether actually outraged by this newfound evidence proving the existence of The Ritual, or a smokescreen intended to deflect any knowledge or responsibility, the studios unilaterally declared that they would not hire any of these "New Radical" Toon actors.

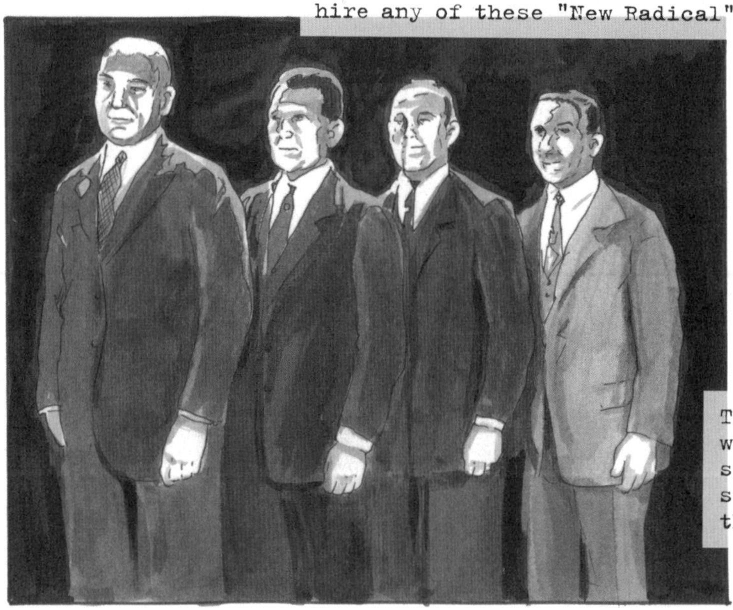

The WARMER BROTHERS were the most outspoken of all the studios on banning these extreme Toons.

Ironically, just sixteen days after the secret meetings were held, Warmer Brothers Studios would sign PORTLY PIG, one of these so-called New Radicals, to a lucrative, long-term contract.

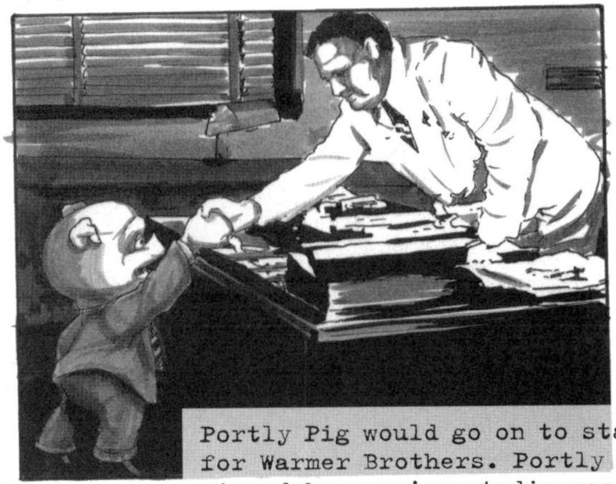

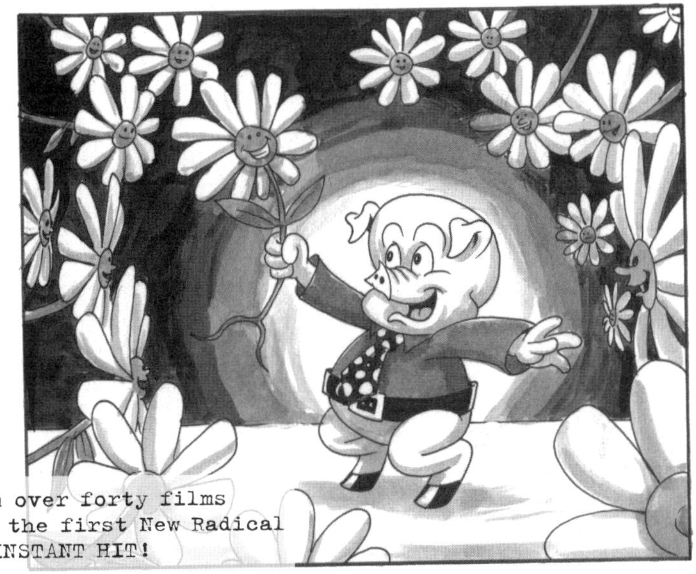

Portly Pig would go on to star in over forty films for Warmer Brothers. Portly Pig, the first New Radical signed by a major studio was an INSTANT HIT!

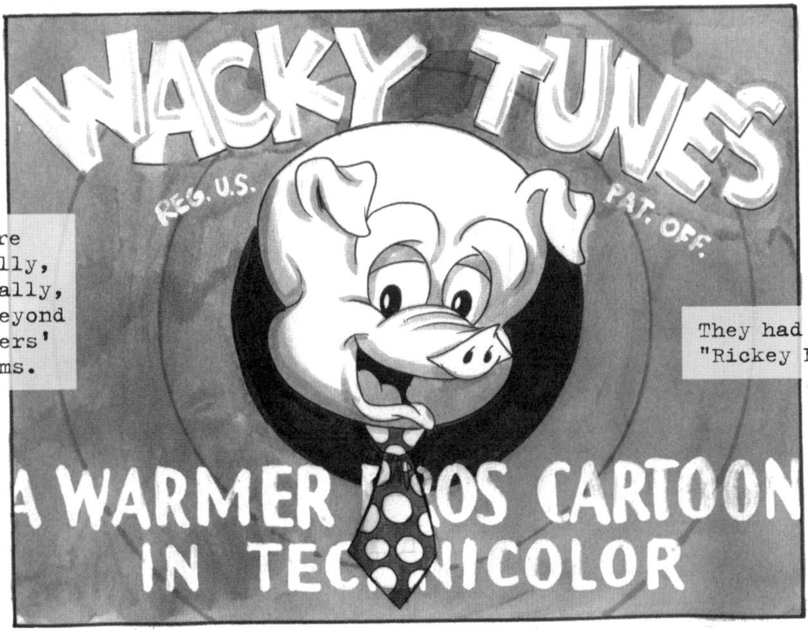
WACKY TUNES
REG. U.S.
PAT. OFF.
A WARMER ROS CARTOON
IN TEC ICOLOR

His films were both critically, and commercially, successful beyond Warmer Brothers' wildest dreams.

They had their "Rickey Rat."

Soon, all Hollywood studios were turning a "blind eye" to what was going on. Their previous condemnation of the New Radicals and The Ritual was quickly forgotten, and the studios began hiring these new, three-fingered stars exclusively.

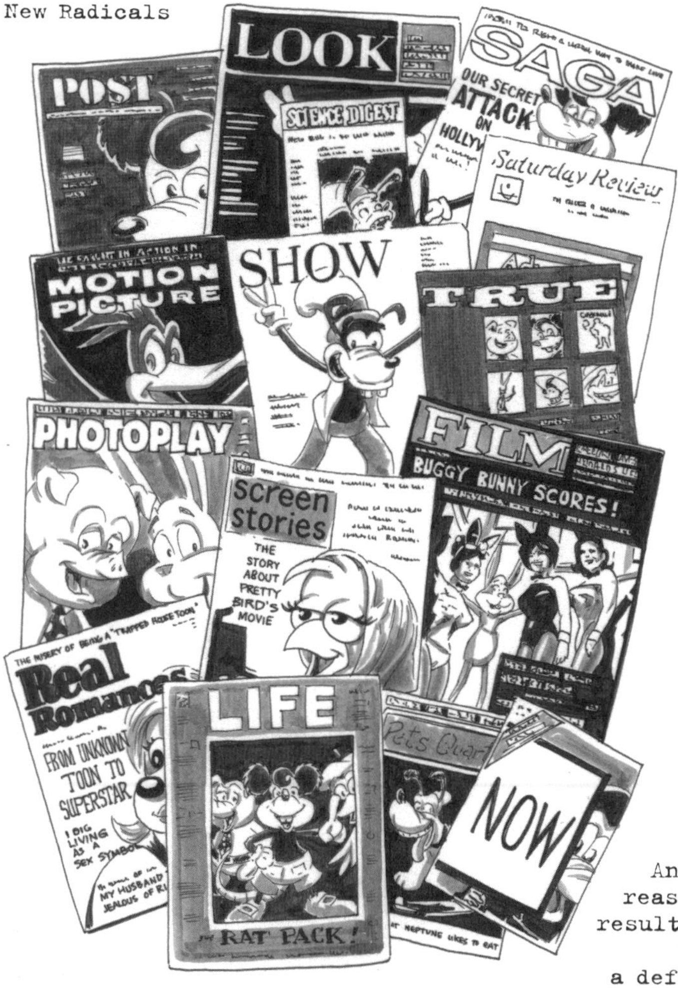
POST
LOOK
SAGA
OUR SECRET ATTACK ON
SCIENCE DIGEST
Saturday Review
MOTION PICTURE
SHOW
TRUE
PHOTOPLAY
FILM
BUGGY BUNNY SCORES!
screen stories
THE STORY ABOUT PRETTY BIRD'S MOVIE
Real Romances
FROM UNKNOWN TOON TO SUPERSTAR
LIFE
RAT PACK!
NOW

Now, it seemed, ONLY the New Radicals were being hired.

And, for whatever reason, whether the results of The Ritual really did have a definite effect or not, these New Radical Toons began to emerge as superstars themselves.

TRIALS & TRIBULATIONS

AFTER PORTLY AND THE OTHERS, INCLUDING MY FATHER, EMERGED AS LEGITIMATE MOVIE-STARS, ALL HELL BROKE LOOSE.
I MEAN THE RITUAL SOON REACHED EPIDEMIC PROPORTIONS.
IT COULDN'T BE IGNORED ANY LONGER.

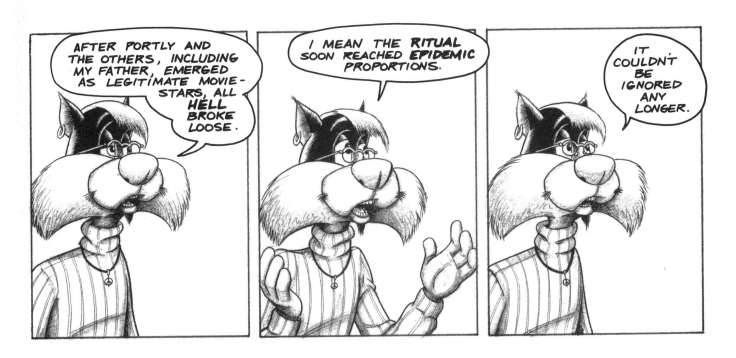

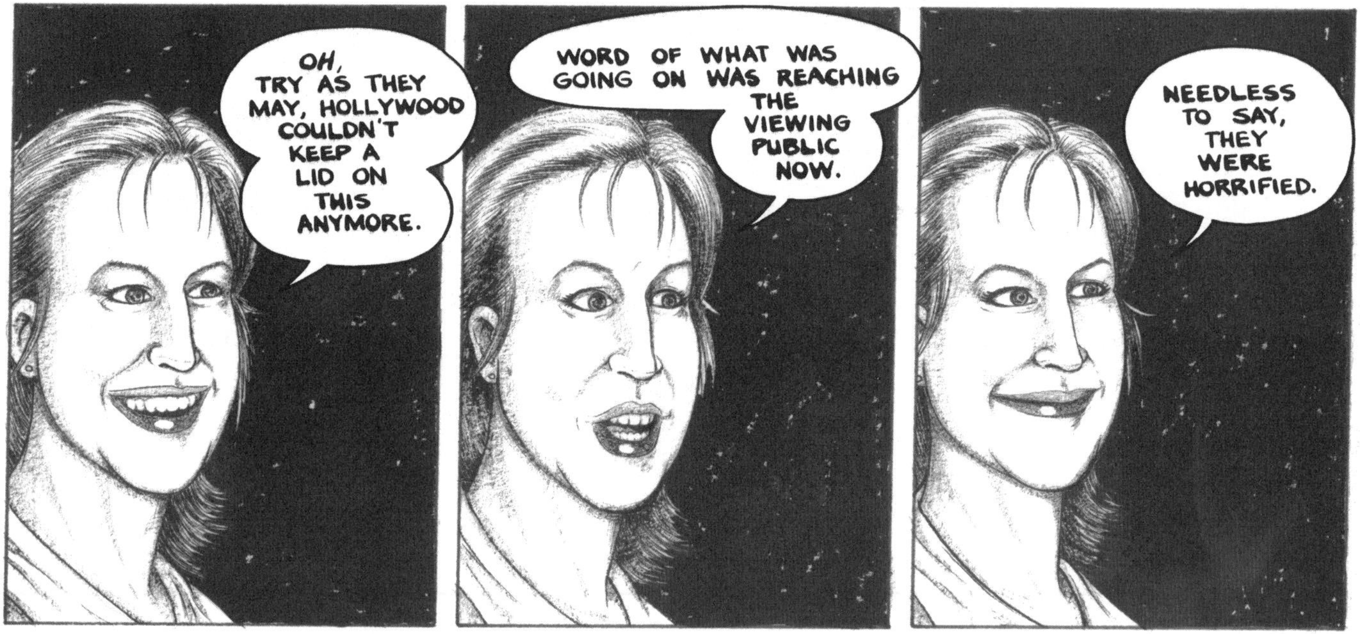
OH, TRY AS THEY MAY, HOLLYWOOD COULDN'T KEEP A LID ON THIS ANYMORE.
WORD OF WHAT WAS GOING ON WAS REACHING THE VIEWING PUBLIC NOW.
NEEDLESS TO SAY, THEY WERE HORRIFIED.

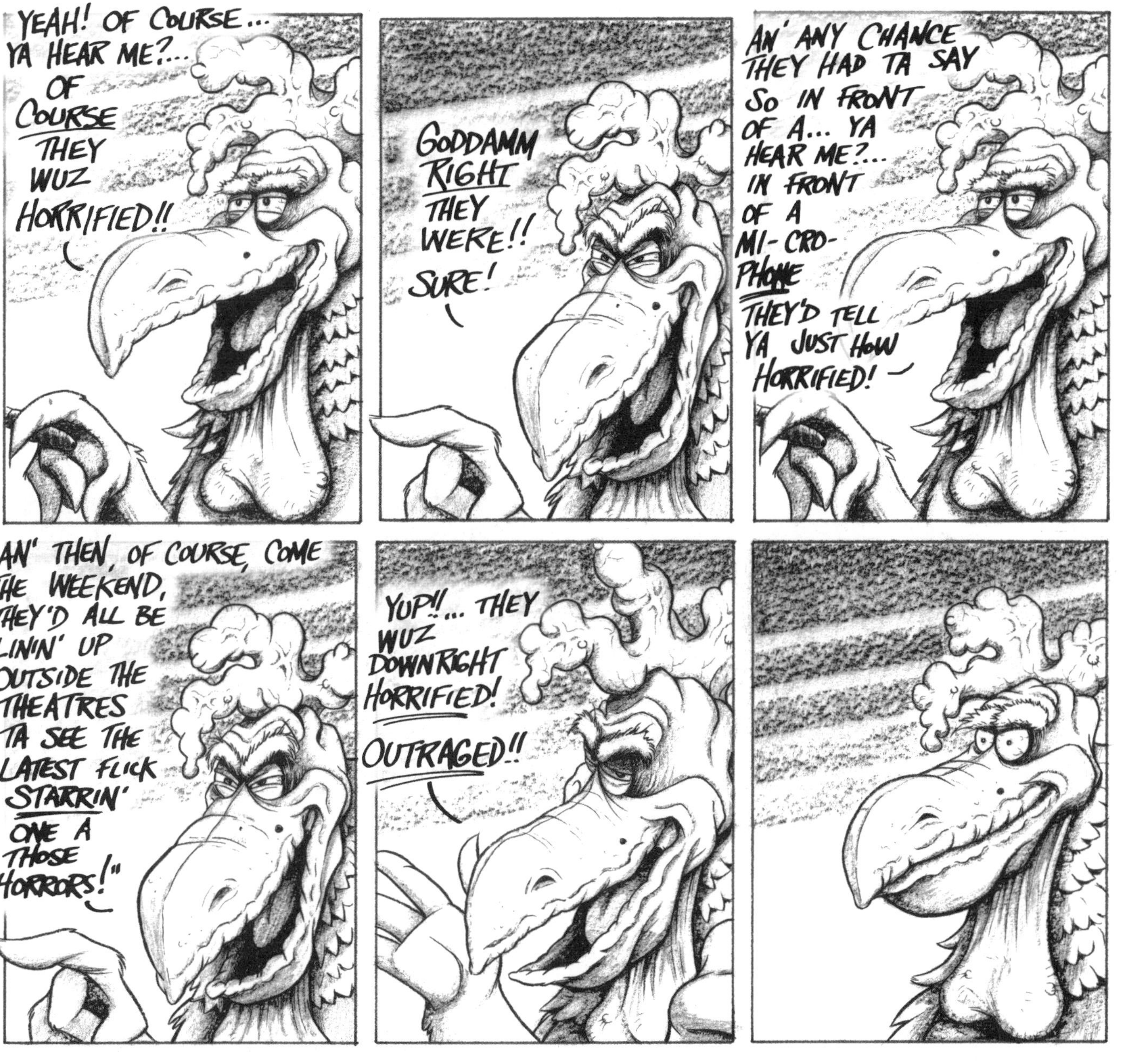
YEAH! OF COURSE... YA HEAR ME?... OF COURSE THEY WUZ HORRIFIED!!
GODDAMM RIGHT THEY WERE!! SURE!
AN' ANY CHANCE THEY HAD TA SAY SO IN FRONT OF A... YA HEAR ME?... IN FRONT OF A MI-CRO-PHONE THEY'D TELL YA JUST HOW HORRIFIED!
AN' THEN, OF COURSE, COME THE WEEKEND, THEY'D ALL BE LININ' UP OUTSIDE THE THEATRES TA SEE THE LATEST FLICK STARRIN' ONE A THOSE "HORRORS!"
YUP!!... THEY WUZ DOWNRIGHT HORRIFIED!
OUTRAGED!!

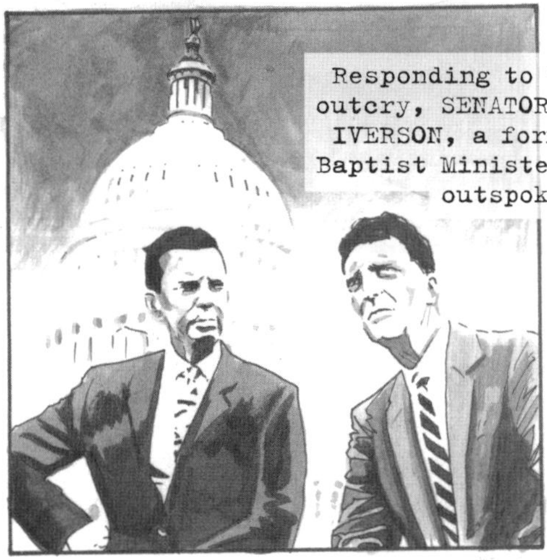
Responding to the public's outcry, SENATOR THEODORE L. IVERSON, a former Missouri Baptist Minister, became an outspoken critic of The Ritual.

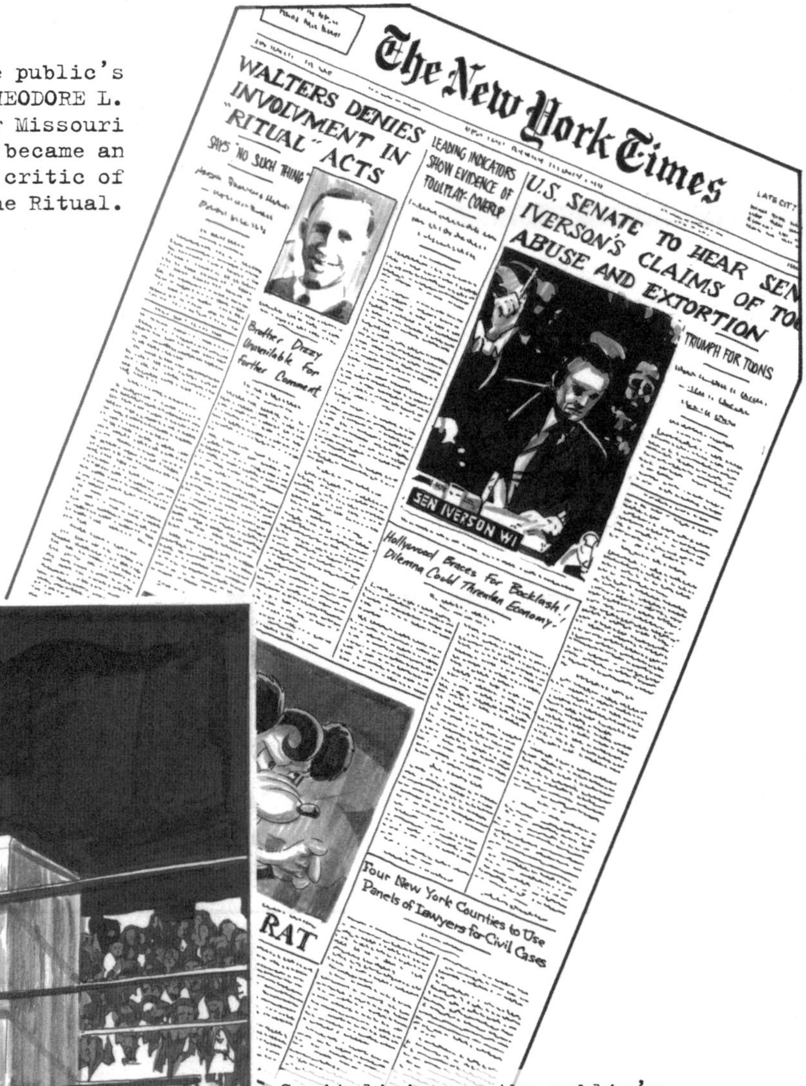
The New York Times
LATE CITY
WALTERS DENIES INVOLVMENT IN "RITUAL" ACTS
SAYS "NO SUCH THING"
LEADING INDICATORS SHOW EVIDENCE OF FOULPLAY: COVERUP
U.S. SENATE TO HEAR SEN IVERSON'S CLAIMS OF TO ABUSE AND EXTORTION
TRIUMPH FOR TOONS
Brother Drezy Unavailable for further Comment
SEN IVERSON WI
Hollywood Braces for Backlash! Dilemma Could Threaten Economy!
RAT
Four New York Counties to Use Panels of Lawyers for Civil Cases

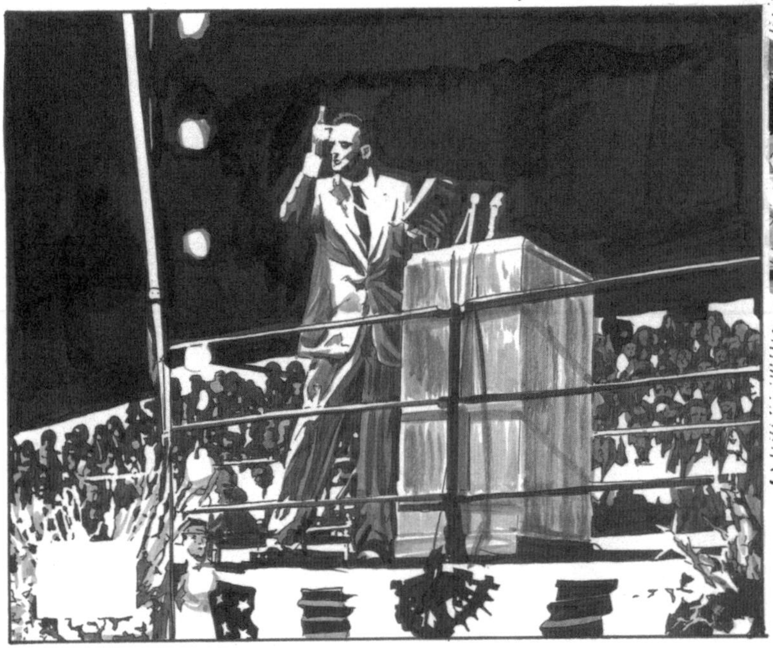

Capitalizing on the public's fear and ignorance, the senator's powerful speeches soon drew him worldwide fame. He would go on to spearhead a movement to outlaw The Ritual.

Senate hearings took place, starting on March 19th, 1951, to determine if this "Ritual" was a violation of Toon Rights. It was a media frenzy. Famous Toons were called to testify, as were top Hollywood producers and directors. It was one of the first "supercases" in U.S. history.

Rickey Rat was called to testify. It was a terrible ordeal for Rickey, as, one by one, he was forced to hear the names and the testimonies of the Toons who mutilated themselves all in the hopes of achieving his type of fame.

Rickey would later say that the guilt he felt during those hearings nearly drove him to suicide.

It was not, however, Rickey who would emerge as the "star witness" in this event, as most expected.

That distinction would fall upon another...

There was one Toon, perhaps more so than all
the others, including Rickey Rat, who reaped
the harvest of the success that cartoons sowed.

Barthalomew Baxter Bunny, the Third: or as
the world would come to know him, BUGGY BUNNY.

Due to a very shrewd talent agent, and
making friends with the right people,
Buggy Bunny achieved notoriety, respect,
and financial success unparalleled
by any other Toon.

And it was HIS TESTIMONY to the Senate,
denying the existence of any cover-up by
Hollywood executives, that most altered
the course of the hearings. Buggy further
denied having personally had this
"so-called Ritual" performed on himself.

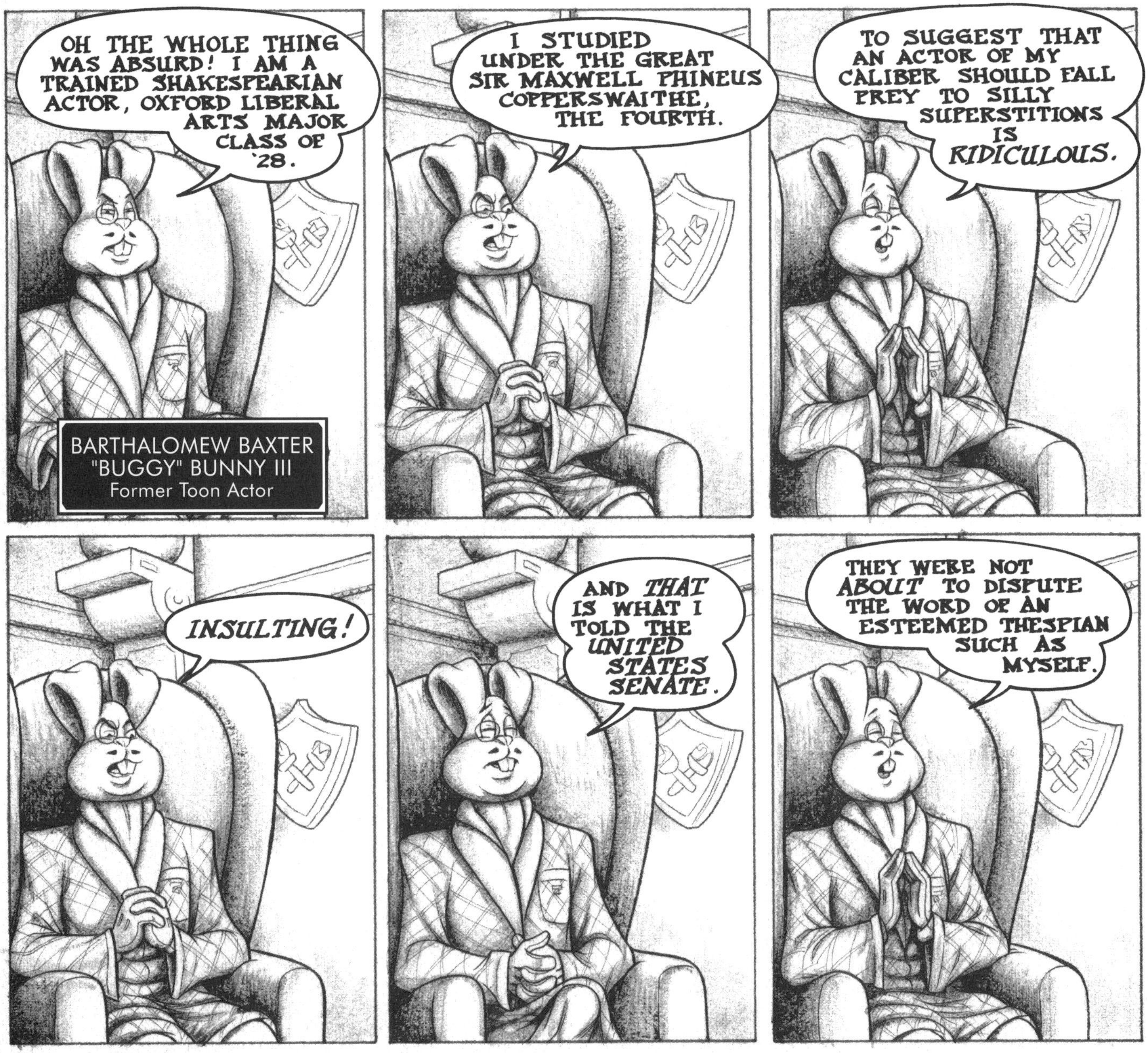
OH THE WHOLE THING WAS ABSURD! I AM A TRAINED SHAKESPEARIAN ACTOR, OXFORD LIBERAL ARTS MAJOR CLASS OF '28.
BARTHALOMEW BAXTER "BUGGY" BUNNY III
Former Toon Actor
I STUDIED UNDER THE GREAT SIR MAXWELL PHINEUS COPPERSWAITHE, THE FOURTH.
TO SUGGEST THAT AN ACTOR OF MY CALIBER SHOULD FALL PREY TO SILLY SUPERSTITIONS IS *RIDICULOUS*.
INSULTING!
AND *THAT* IS WHAT I TOLD THE *UNITED STATES SENATE*.
THEY WERE NOT *ABOUT* TO DISPUTE THE WORD OF AN ESTEEMED THESPIAN SUCH AS MYSELF.

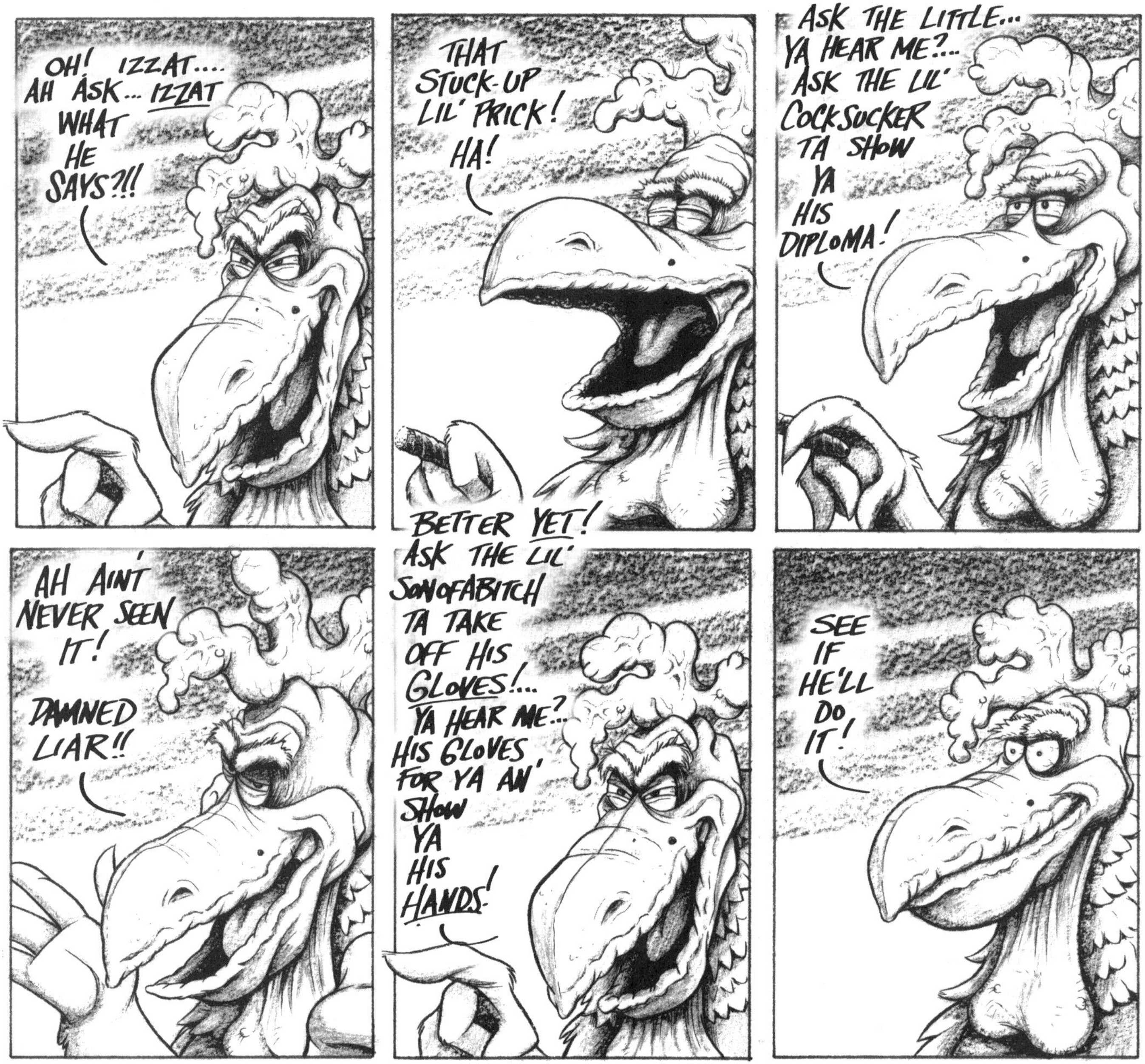
OH! IZZAT.... AH ASK... IZZAT WHAT HE SAYS?!!
THAT STUCK-UP LIL' PRICK! HA!
ASK THE LITTLE... YA HEAR ME?... ASK THE LIL' COCKSUCKER TA SHOW YA HIS DIPLOMA!
AH AIN'T NEVER SEEN IT! DAMNED LIAR!!
BETTER YET! ASK THE LIL' SONOFABITCH TA TAKE OFF HIS GLOVES!... YA HEAR ME?... HIS GLOVES FOR YA AN' SHOW YA HIS HANDS!
SEE IF HE'LL DO IT!

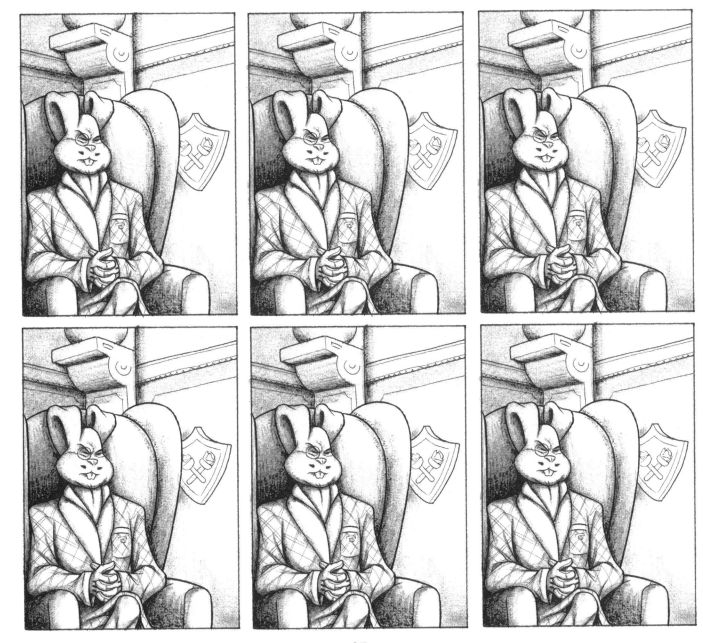

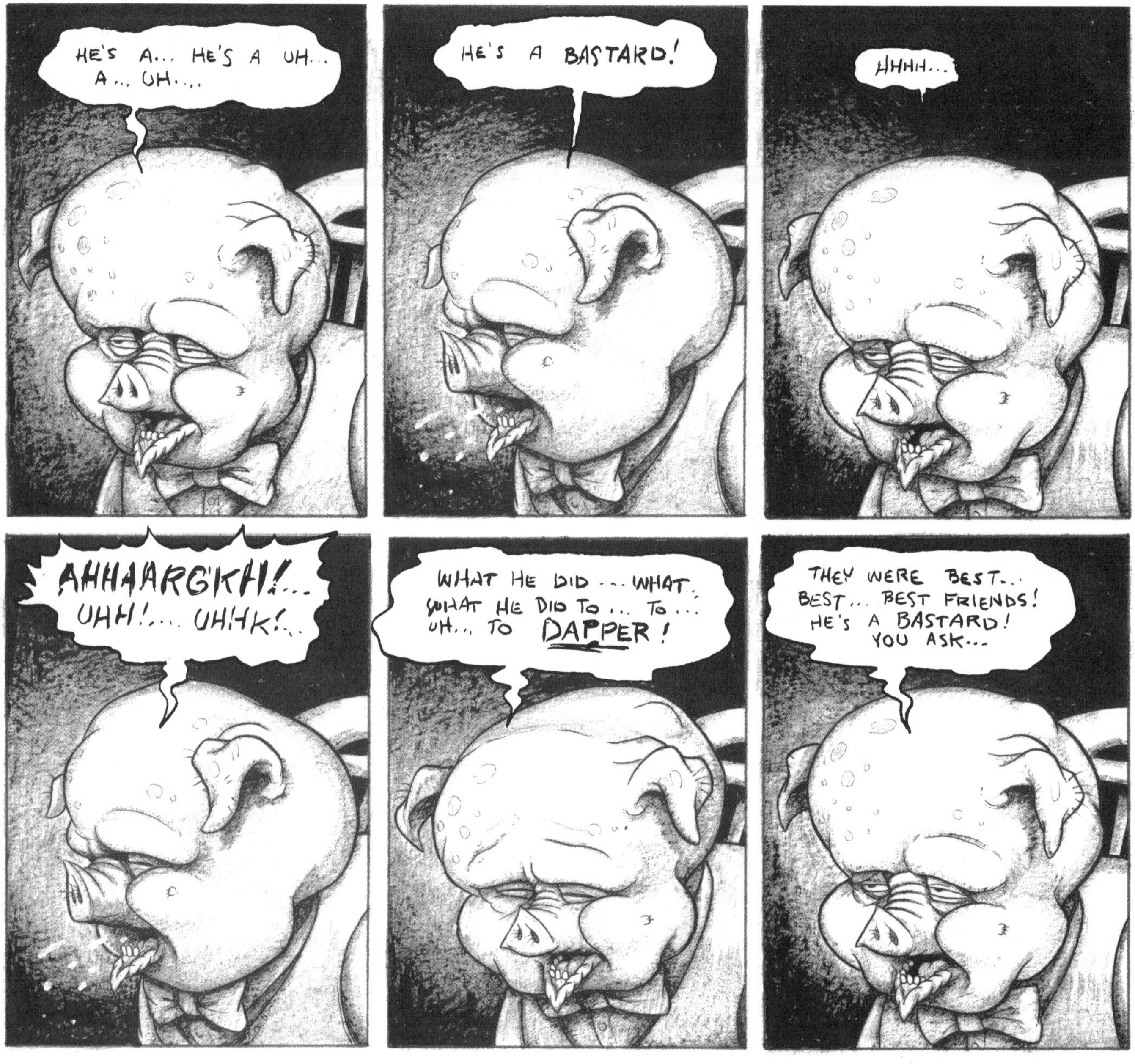
HE'S A... HE'S A UH... A... UH....
HE'S A BASTARD!
UHHH...
AHHAARGKH!... UHH!... UHHK!...
WHAT HE DID... WHAT... WHAT HE DID TO... TO... UH... TO DAPPER!
THEY WERE BEST... BEST... BEST FRIENDS! HE'S A BASTARD! YOU ASK...

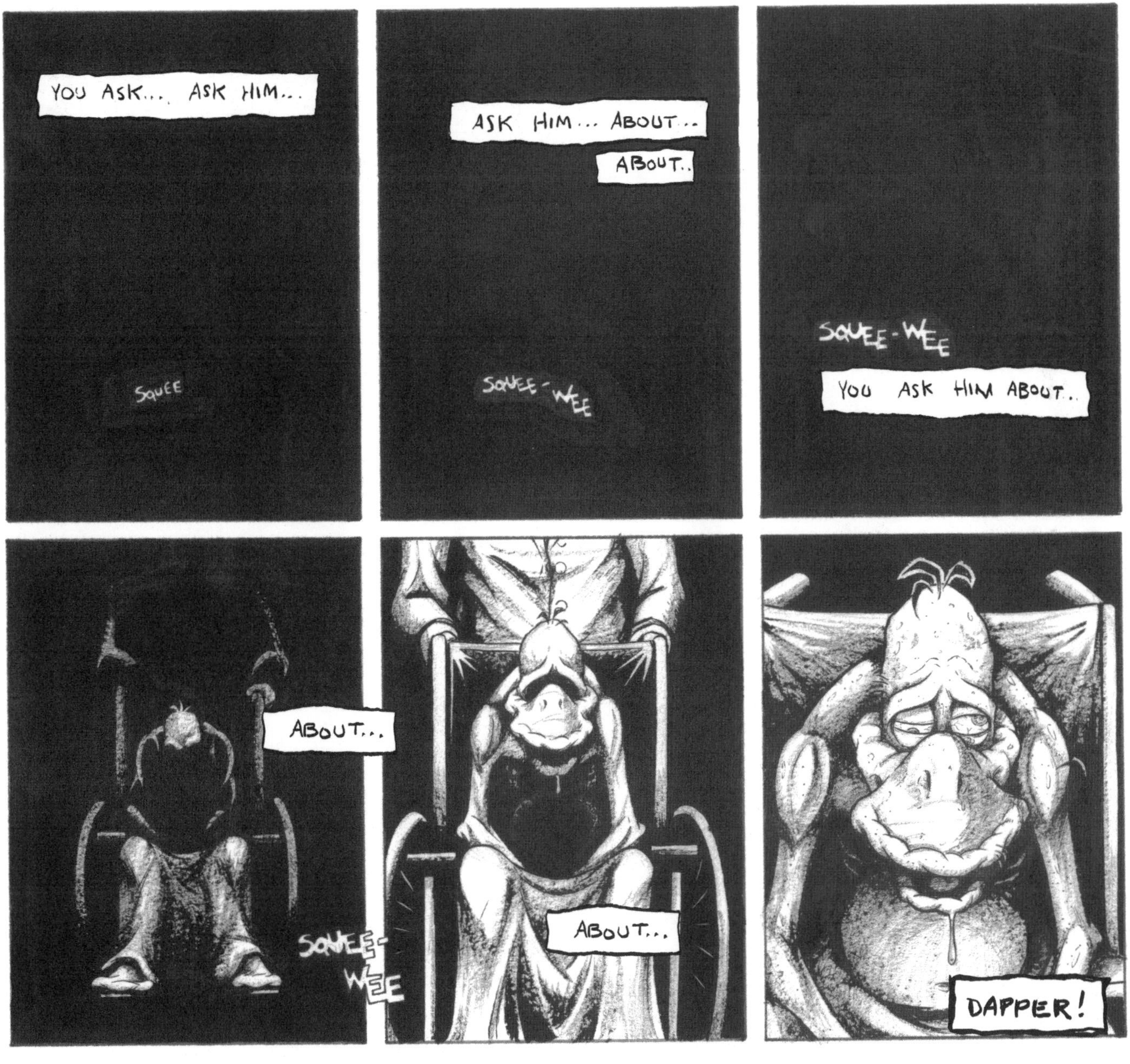

YOU ASK... ASK HIM...
SQUEE
ASK HIM... ABOUT...
ABOUT..
SQUEE-WEE
SQUEE-WEE
YOU ASK HIM ABOUT..
ABOUT...
SQUEE-WEE
ABOUT...
DAPPER!

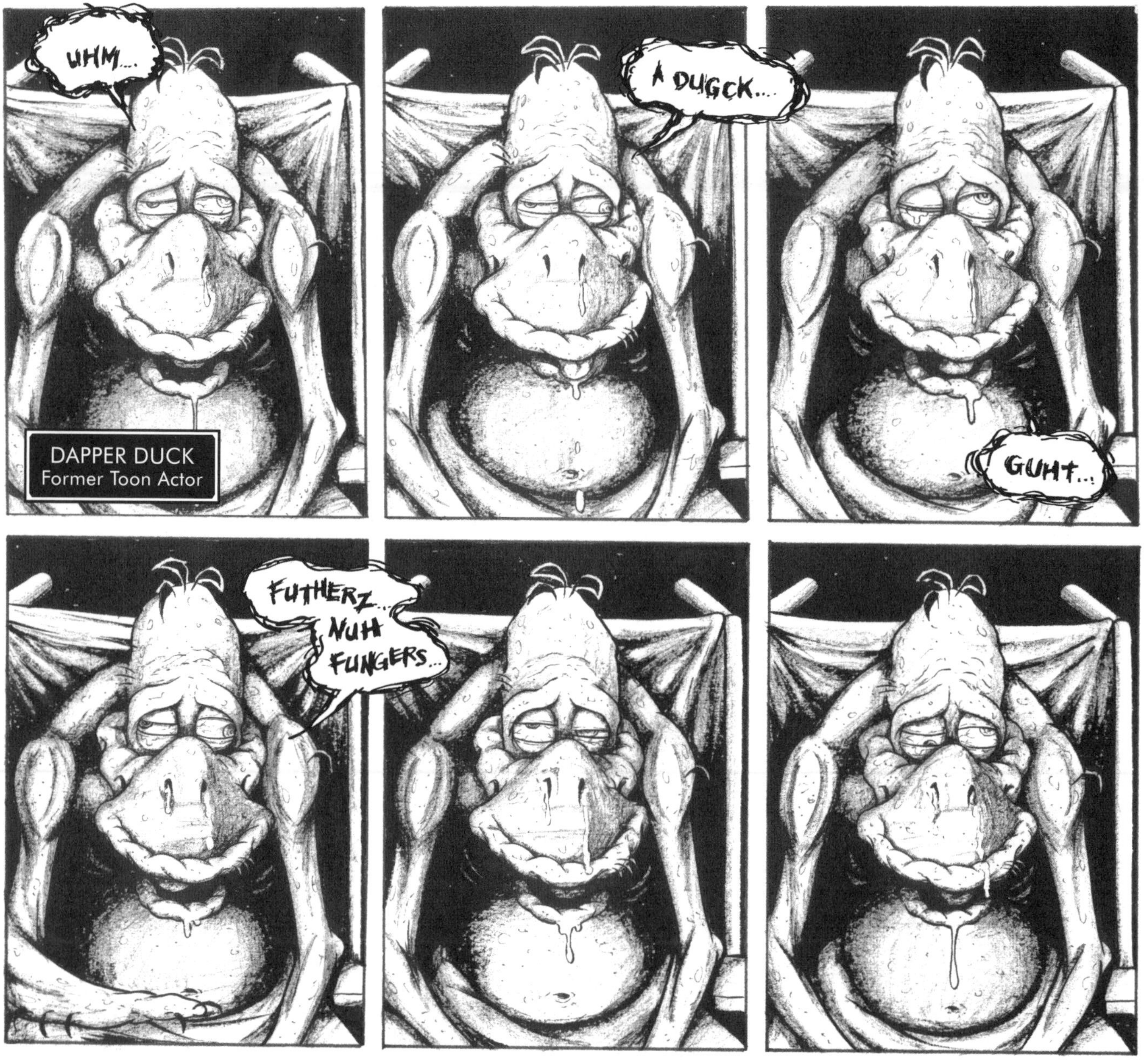
UHM...
DAPPER DUCK
Former Toon Actor
A DUGCK...
GUHT...
FUTHERZ... NUH FUNGERS...

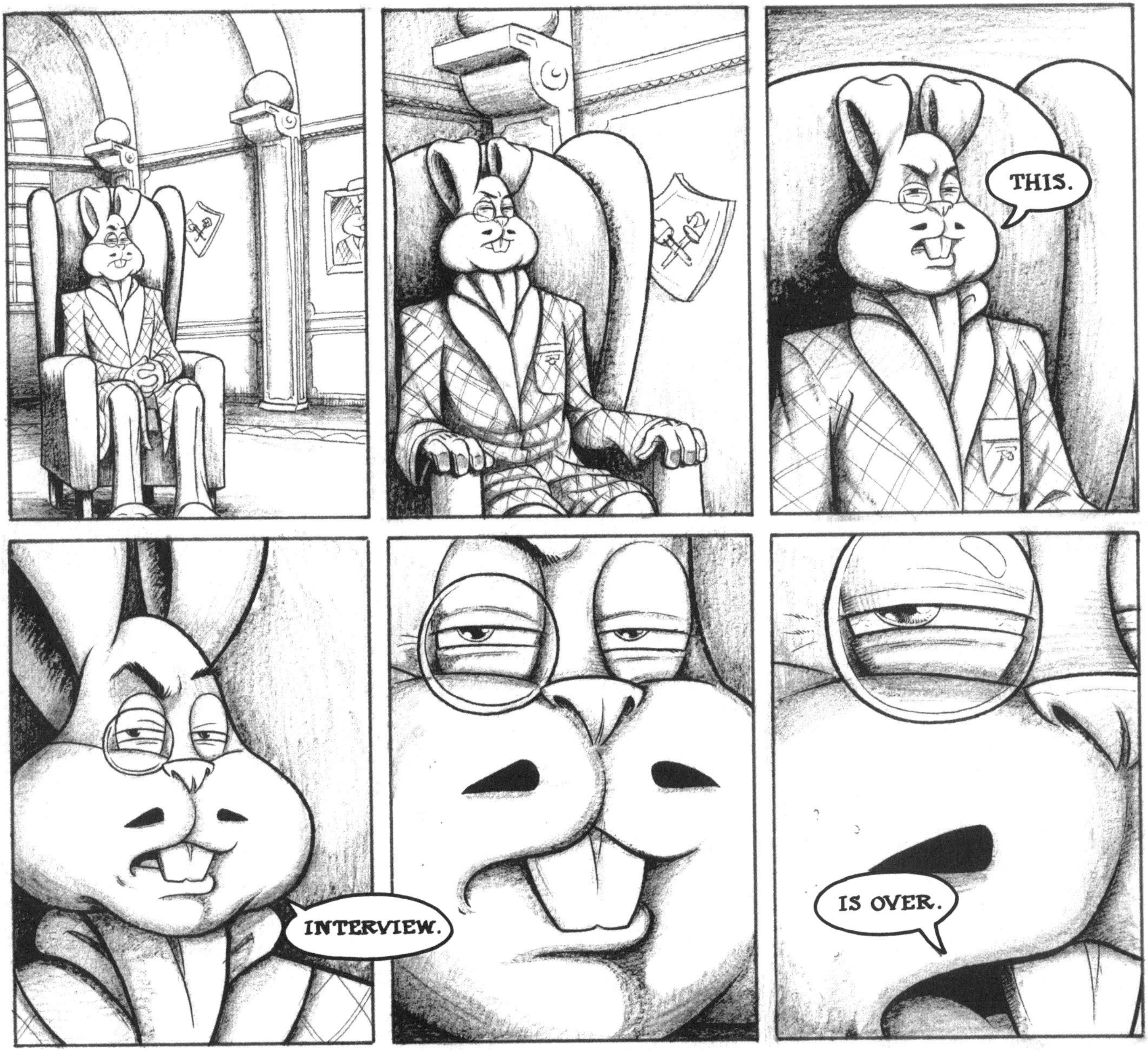
THIS.
INTERVIEW.
IS OVER.

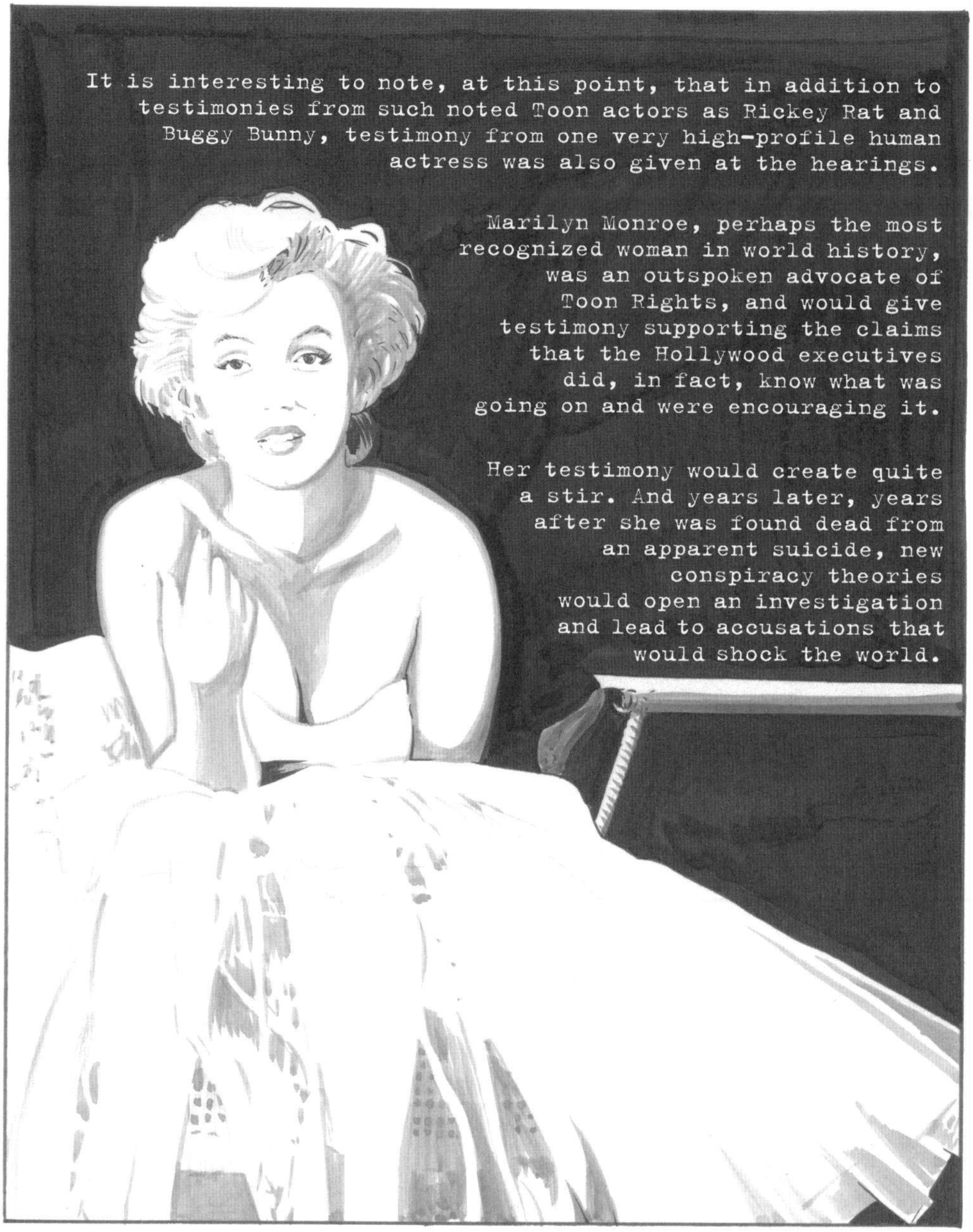
It is interesting to note, at this point, that in addition to testimonies from such noted Toon actors as Rickey Rat and Buggy Bunny, testimony from one very high-profile human actress was also given at the hearings.
Marilyn Monroe, perhaps the most recognized woman in world history, was an outspoken advocate of Toon Rights, and would give testimony supporting the claims that the Hollywood executives did, in fact, know what was going on and were encouraging it.
Her testimony would create quite a stir. And years later, years after she was found dead from an apparent suicide, new conspiracy theories would open an investigation and lead to accusations that would shock the world.

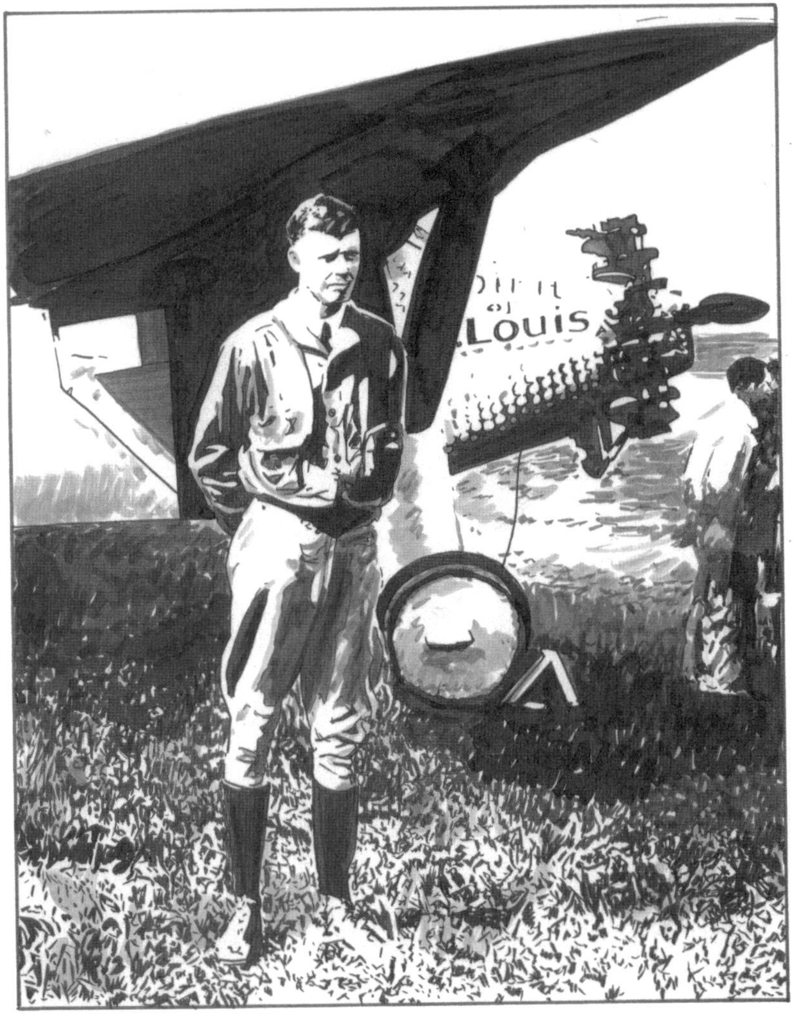
Louis

Throughout the years, many high-profile celebrities and political leaders would speak out against the abuse and mistreatment of Toons.

They would use their celebrity status to draw attention to this very real problem.

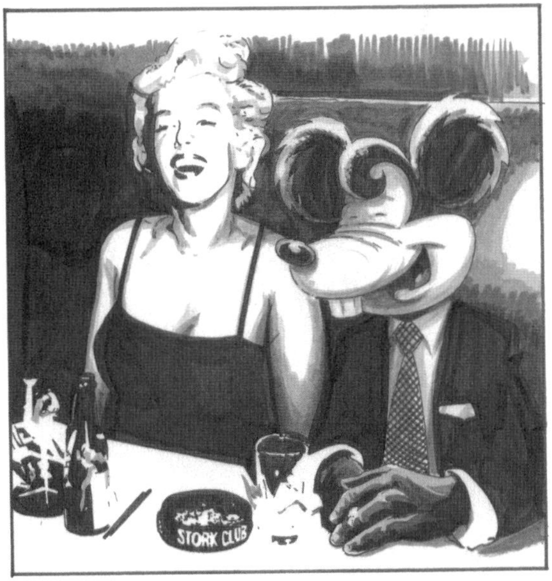
STORK CLUB

By doing so, they would be
revered by the Toon community,
and often strike up life-long
friendships in the process.

Unfortunately, by speaking out, they would also make some very powerful enemies.

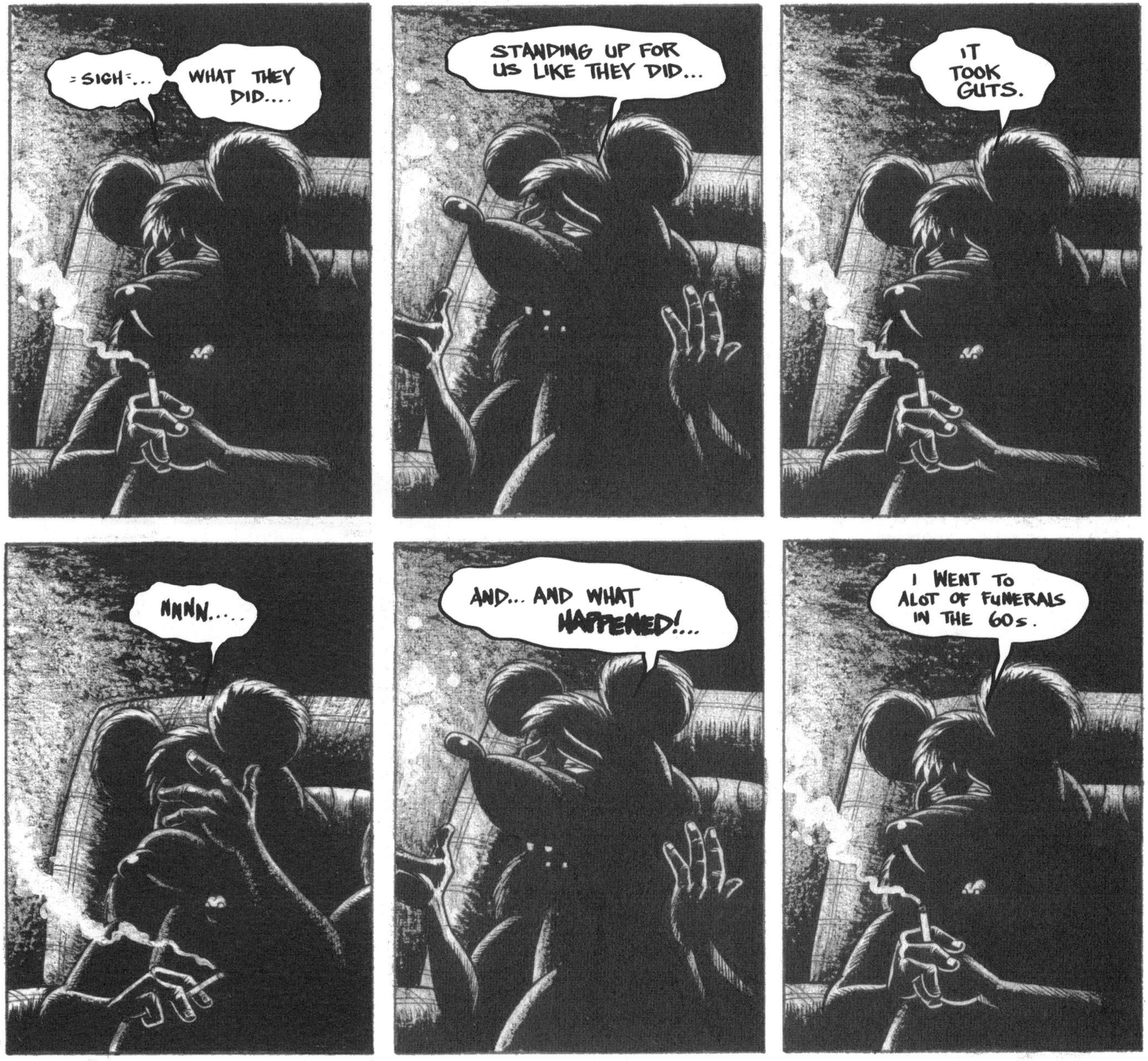

=SIGH=... WHAT THEY DID....
STANDING UP FOR US LIKE THEY DID...
IT TOOK GUTS.
MMMN.....
AND... AND WHAT HAPPENED!...
I WENT TO ALOT OF FUNERALS IN THE 60s.

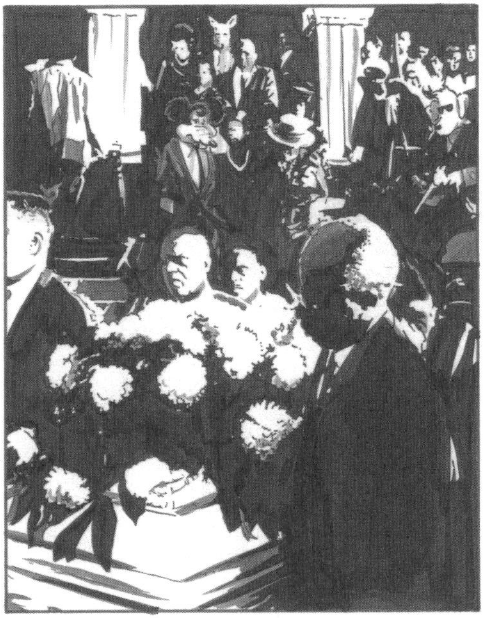

Whether as a result of their speaking out on behalf of Toon Rights, or not, the most high-profile of all the celebrities to do so would suffer horrible, mysterious fates.

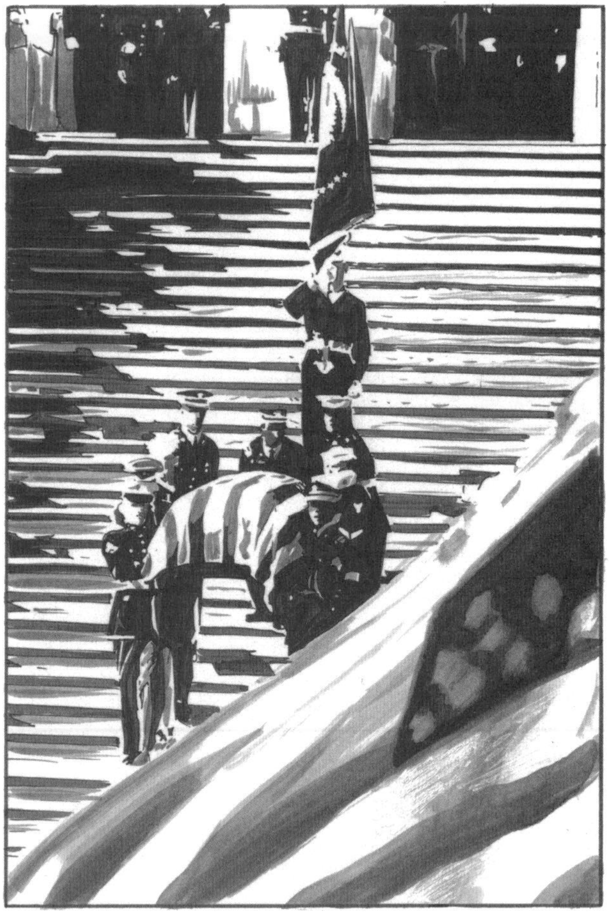

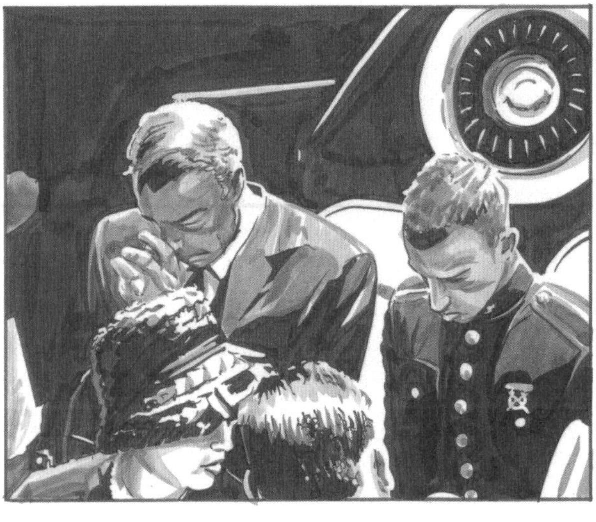

And although at the times of these terrible tragedies no immediate connections were made, in the years to come, some investigators would claim the victims' prior outspoken support of Toon Rights an undeniable common thread.

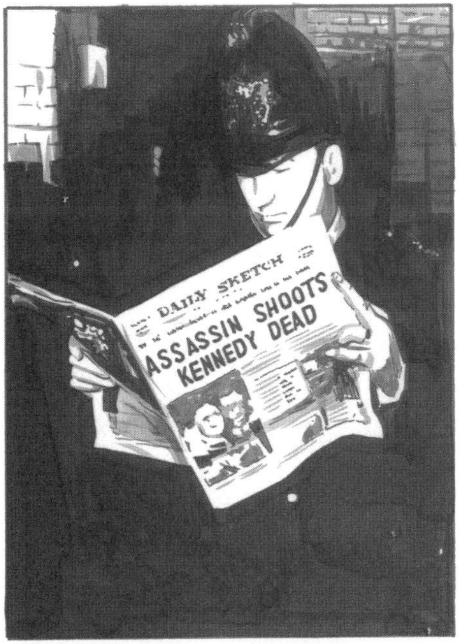
DAILY SKETCH
ASSASSIN SHOOTS KENNEDY DEAD

A common thread that would have conspiracy theorists debating for decades to come.

Many questions would be asked regarding a possible connection. Was there, indeed, a COMMON THREAD?

Were these celebrity tragedies the result of some cruel vendetta? And, if so, who was responsible?

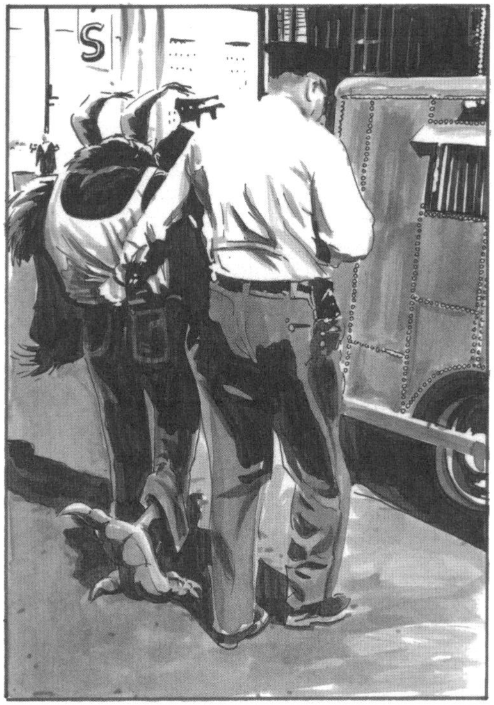

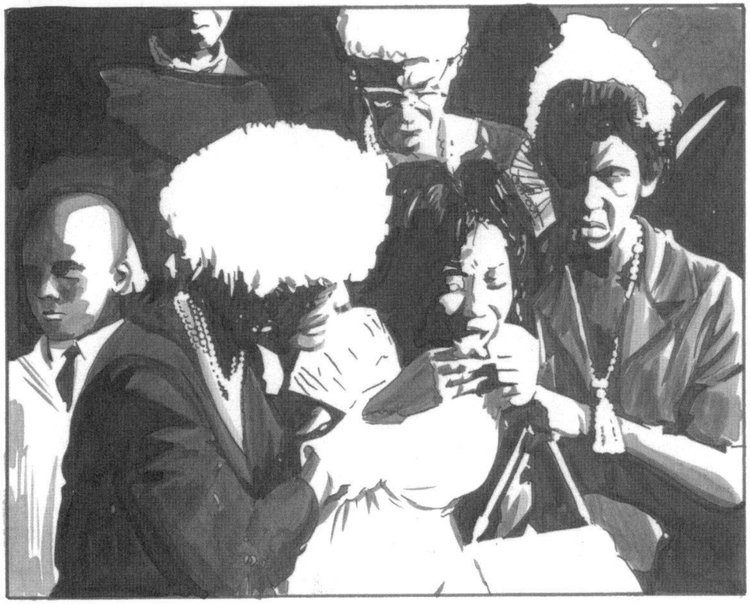

Some would claim it was Hollywood...

Some a "lone Toon gunman"--
A radical Toon counter-revolutionary...

Some would go so far as to claim that the vendetta would continue on, and that, as a result, future generations would also, unfortunately, suffer the "sins of the father."

But, some ten years before Marilyn Monroe's mysterious death, and the similarly controversial deaths of other historical figures, was her testimony to the Senate in March of 1951.

It was, perhaps, her testimony, more so than any other's, that finally forced Hollywood's hand.

Embarrassed by all the negative publicity and accusatorial speculations generated by the hearings, Hollywood had no choice but to finally stop turning a blind eye as to what was happening and put an end to The Ritual once and for all.

They showed a unified front and publicly condemned The Ritual, and together with the U.S. Senate, they drafted into law measures that would cost dearly any medical professional caught performing the procedure on any new Toons.

And finally, the mutilation stopped.

95

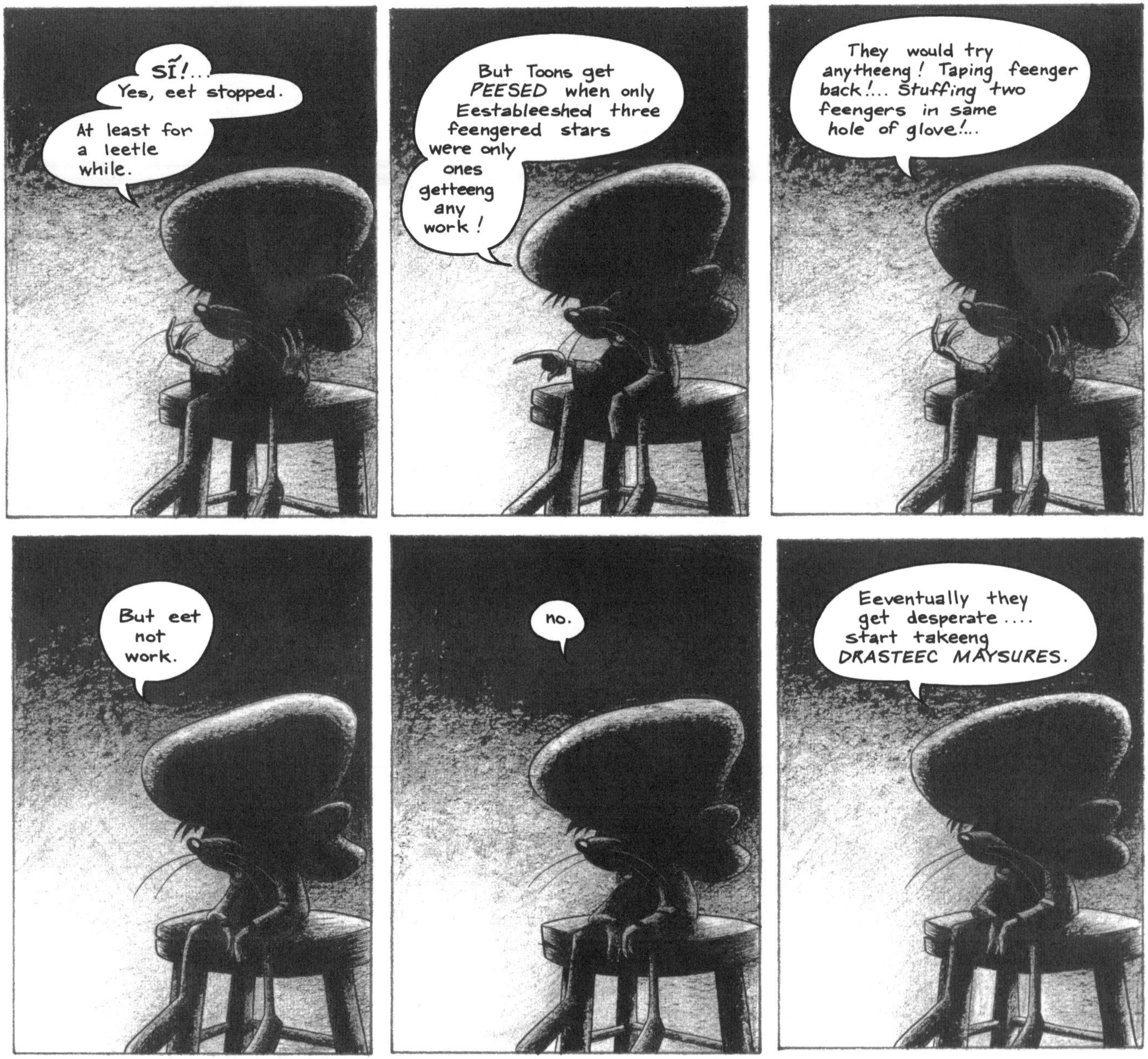
SÍ!... Yes, eet stopped.
At least for a leetle while.
But Toons get PEESED when only Eestableeshed three feengered stars were only ones getteeng any work!
They would try anytheeng! Taping feenger back!... Stuffing two feengers in same hole of glove!...
But eet not work.
no.
Eeventually they get desperate.... start takeeng DRASTEEC MAYSURES.

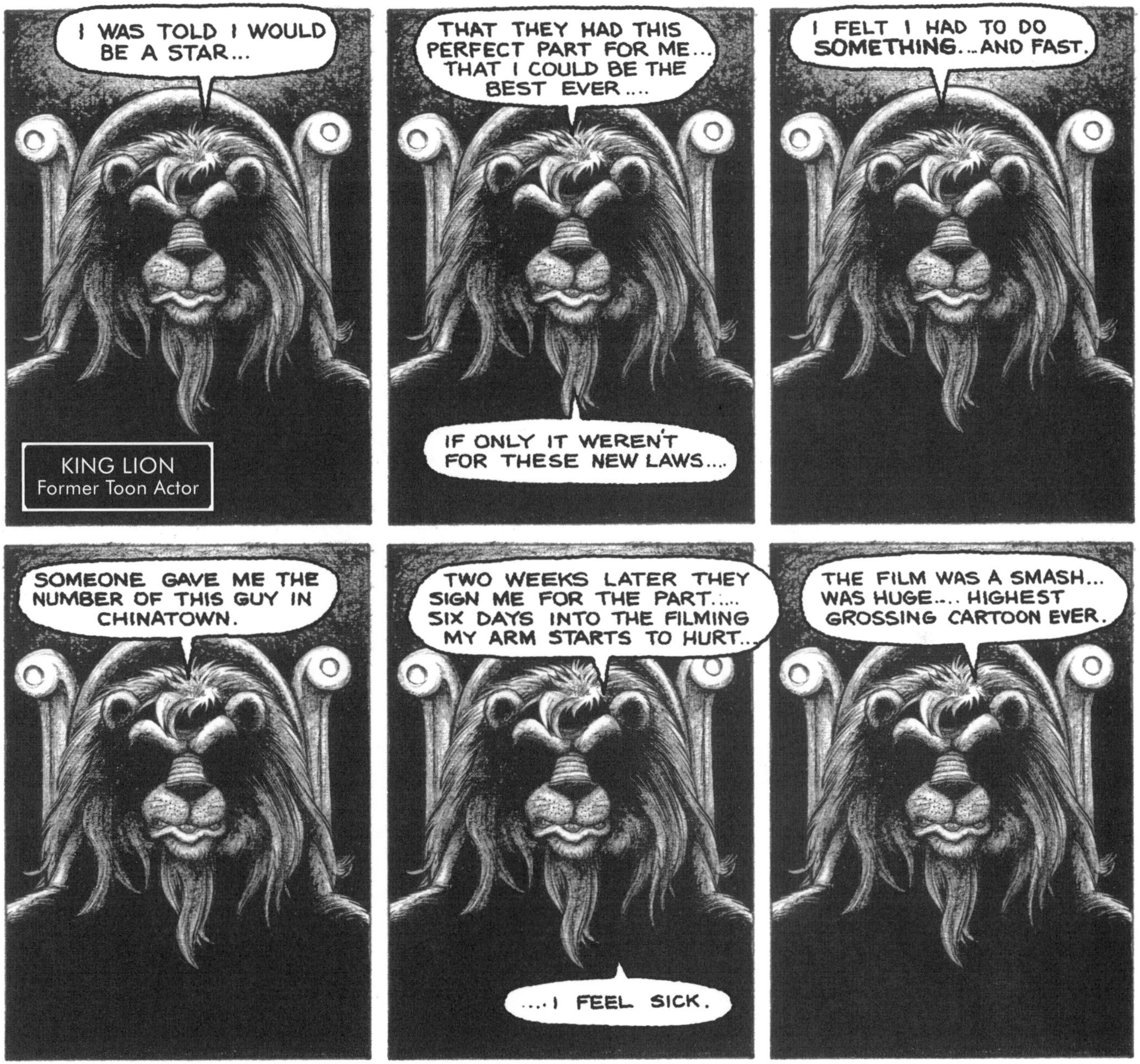
I WAS TOLD I WOULD BE A STAR...
KING LION
Former Toon Actor
THAT THEY HAD THIS PERFECT PART FOR ME... THAT I COULD BE THE BEST EVER....
IF ONLY IT WEREN'T FOR THESE NEW LAWS....
I FELT I HAD TO DO SOMETHING...AND FAST.
SOMEONE GAVE ME THE NUMBER OF THIS GUY IN CHINATOWN.
TWO WEEKS LATER THEY SIGN ME FOR THE PART..... SIX DAYS INTO THE FILMING MY ARM STARTS TO HURT...
....I FEEL SICK.
THE FILM WAS A SMASH... WAS HUGE.... HIGHEST GROSSING CARTOON EVER.

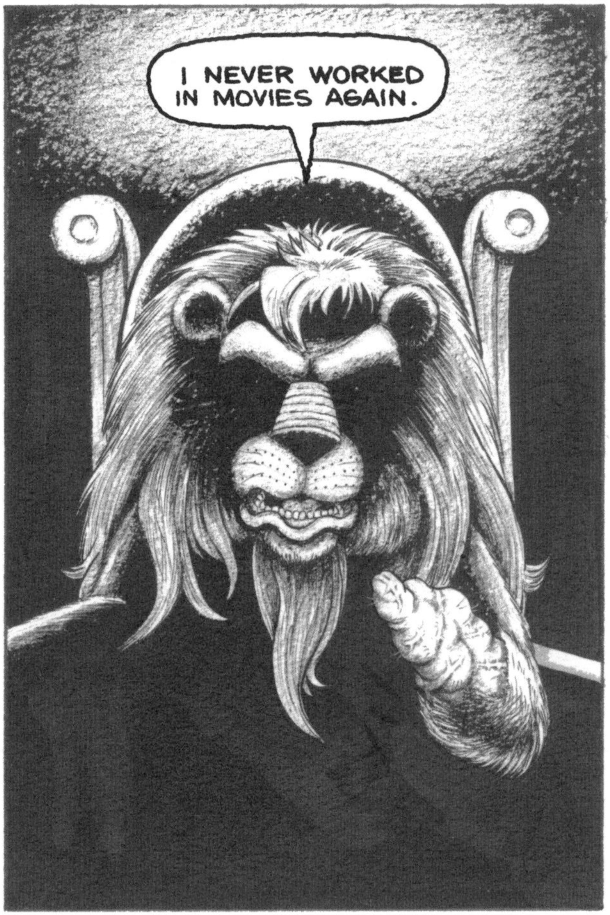
I NEVER WORKED IN MOVIES AGAIN.

NOBODY WAS FORCING THEM.
NO ONE.

AND AS I'VE STATED BEFORE WE WERE NOT CONDONING THIS!

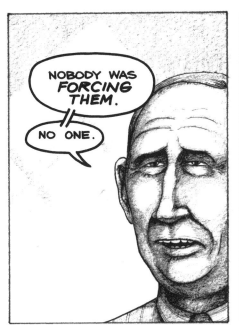

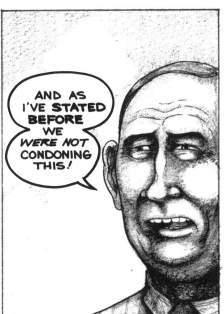

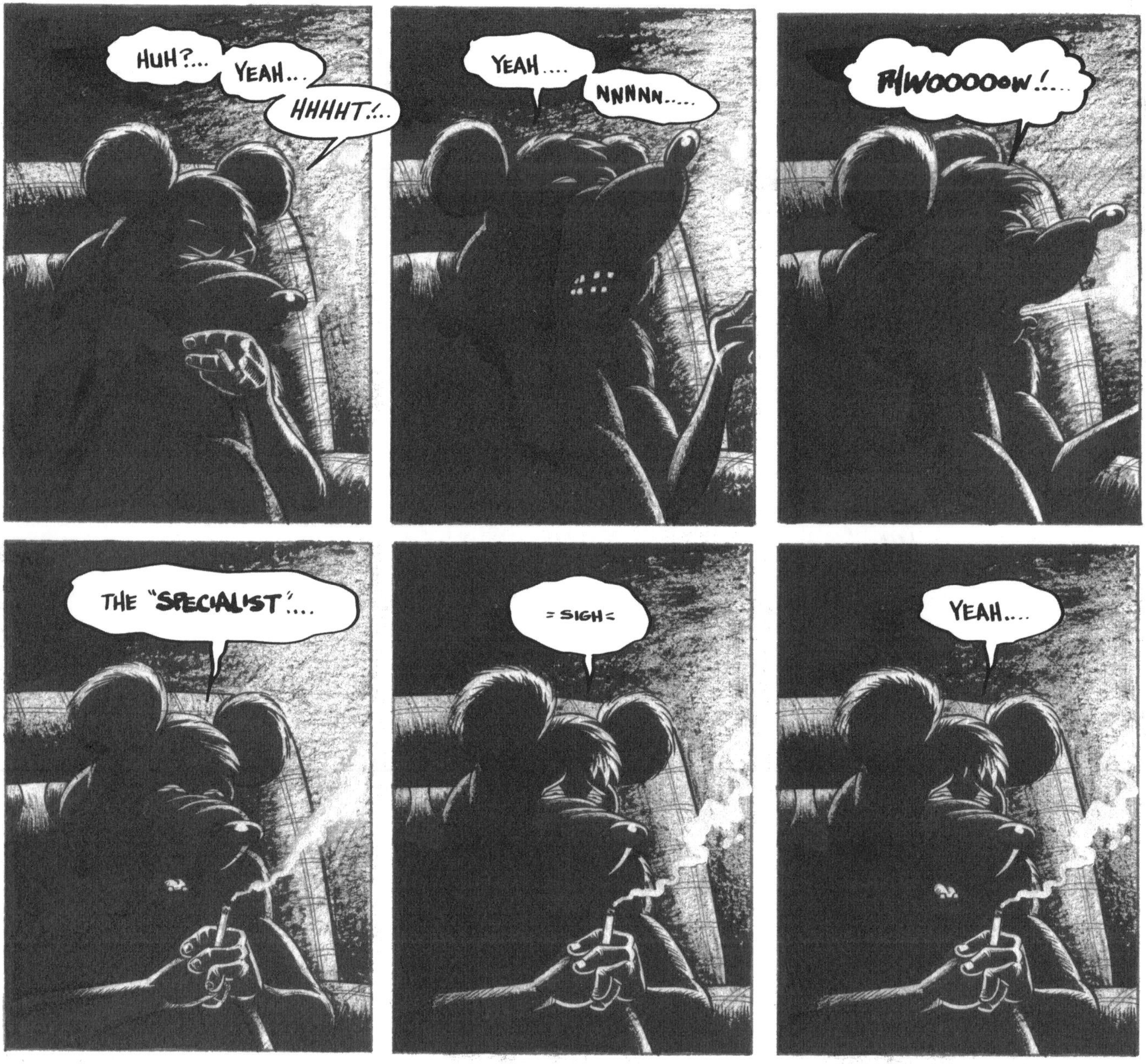
HUH?...
YEAH...
HHHHT!...
YEAH....
NNNNN.....
PHWOOOOOOW!....
THE "SPECIALIST"....
= SIGH =
YEAH....

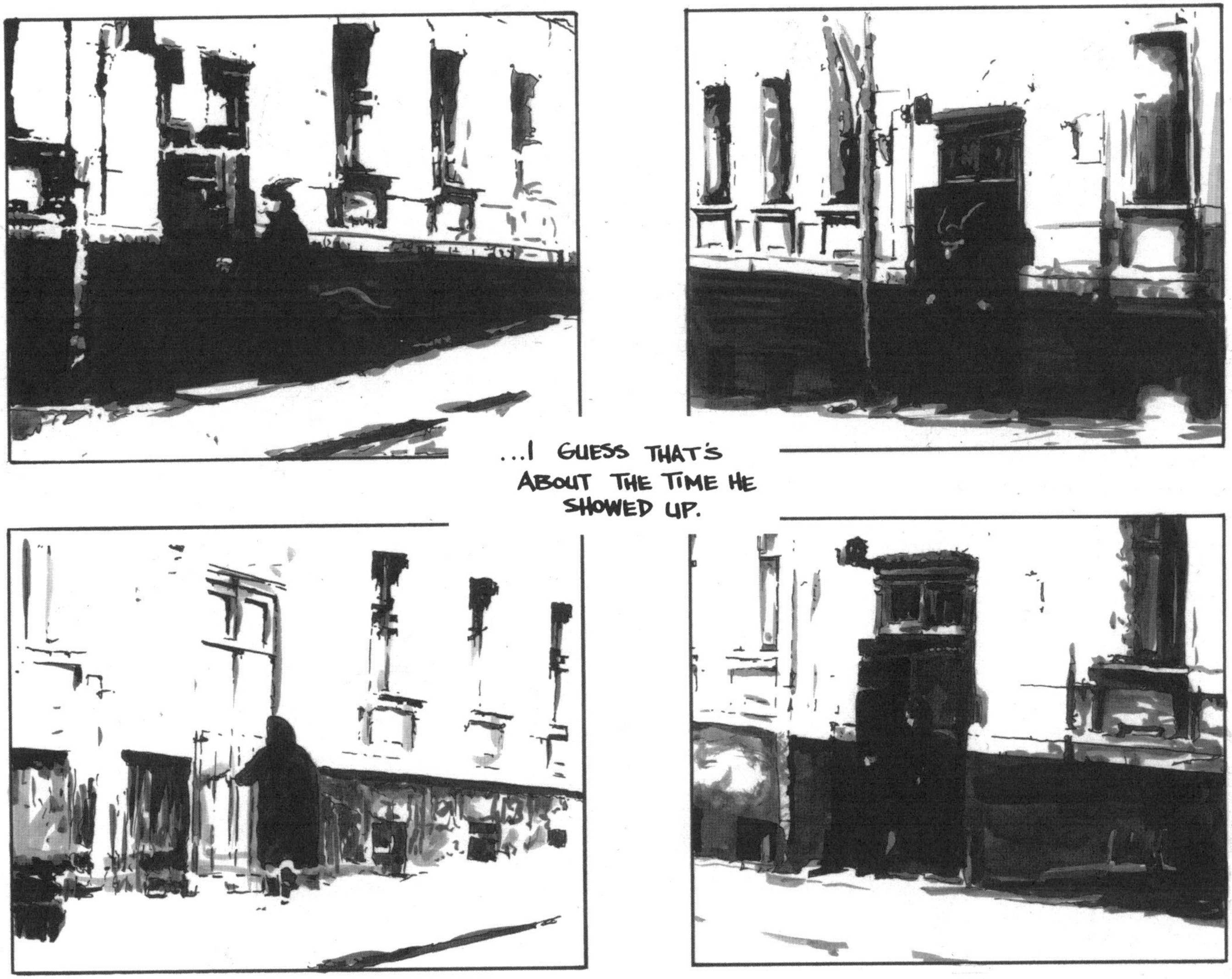
...I GUESS THAT'S ABOUT THE TIME HE SHOWED UP.

THE SPECIALIST

HAH! SCHPECIALIST!...
JA!...
I DO NOT ZAY FOR SHUAH EEF ZIS ZO-CALLED "SCHPECIALIST" EXISTED, OR NOT.
I SINK IT MAKE FOR GOOT SHTORYTELLING THOUGH, NO?

OF COURSE THE SPECIALIST WAS REAL.
THE EVIDENCE OF HIS EXISTENCE IS IRREFUTABLE.
ONE *CANNOT* DENY THE FACTS.

FACTS ?! WHAT FACTS ?!!
IT'S RIDICULOUS!...
I'VE NEVER SEEN ANY EVIDENCE SUPPORTING THIS... THIS MYTH!
AND THAT IS EXACTLY WHAT IT IS....
A MYTH!

WELL NOW... YA HEAR ME?... NOW WE'RE GETTIN' SOMEWHERE!
OKAY, AH'LL PLAY ALONG... YA HEAR ME?... AH SAID AH'LL PLAY ALONG!..
NAWWW!... AH AIN'T NEVER HEARD A HIM! HEH HEH HEH...

Just a few short years after laws were passed banning the act of The Ritual, an unidentified man would surface, and once again, controversy and carnage would surround the cartoon industry.

His identity, though often speculated upon, would never truly become revealed.
He would simply come to be known as "The Specialist."

This photo is one of only a handful known to exist, capturing The Specialist posing as a photographer at a California Bikini Contest. Because of his location in the far background, even enlargements fail to give an accurate representation of his features, making it impossible to ascertain his identity.

Although there are very few facts regarding his identity, it is believed that The Specialist was an active participant at the Toon Pro-Choice Rallies that took place during the Senate hearings.

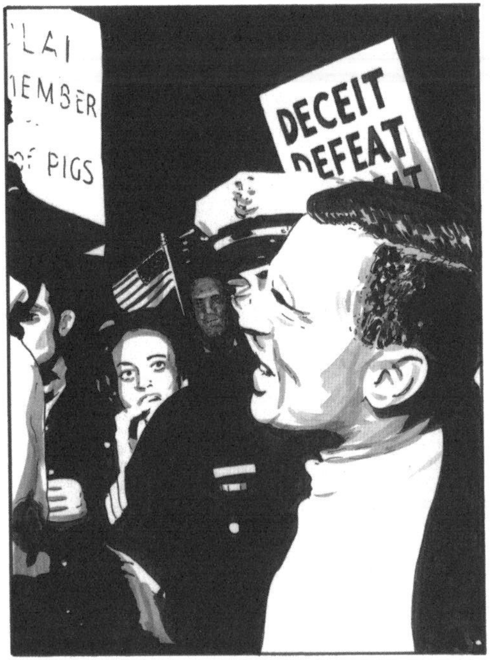
DECEIT
DEFEAT
PIGS

It seems this young activist cleverly devised a way to perform The Ritual surgically, and then falsify the patients' birth records, so that it appeared the Toon was born that way.

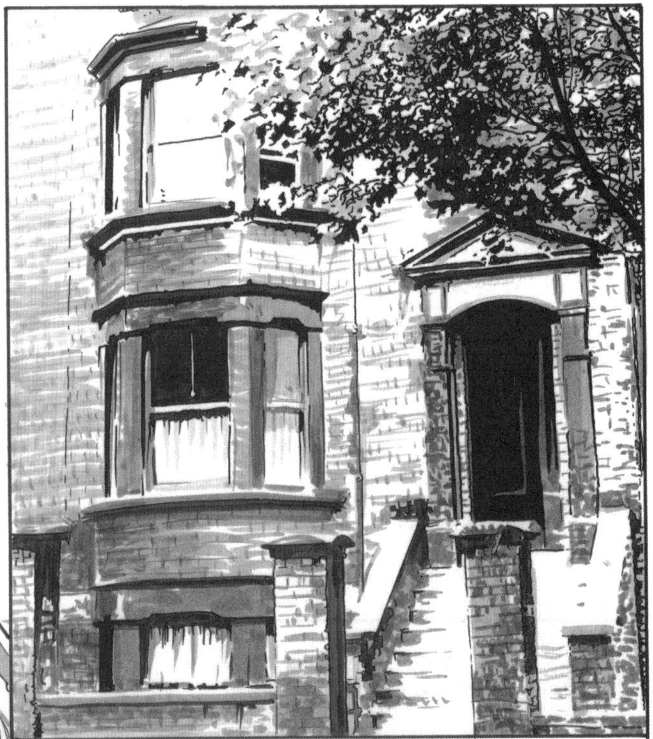

Because of far looser governing, the Toons' health records weren't as closely scrutinized as humans'...

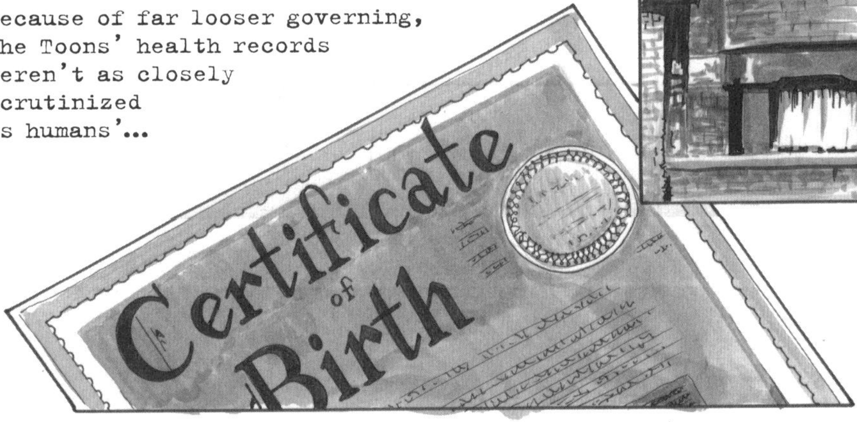
Certificate of Birth

... and it was, apparently, a fairly simple task to get away with.

It seems The Specialist only operated for a very short period of time, perhaps a year, before word got out of his activities. An investigation quickly ensued, but it was too late.

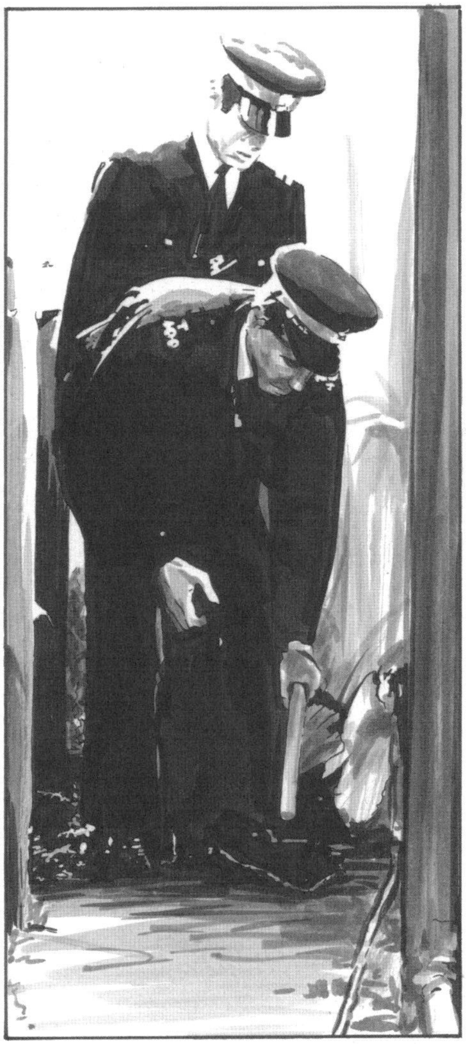

He was gone.

Disappeared.

Little, if any, evidence was discovered during the course of the investigation. Nothing investigators could, with any degree of certainty, positively link to The Specialist.

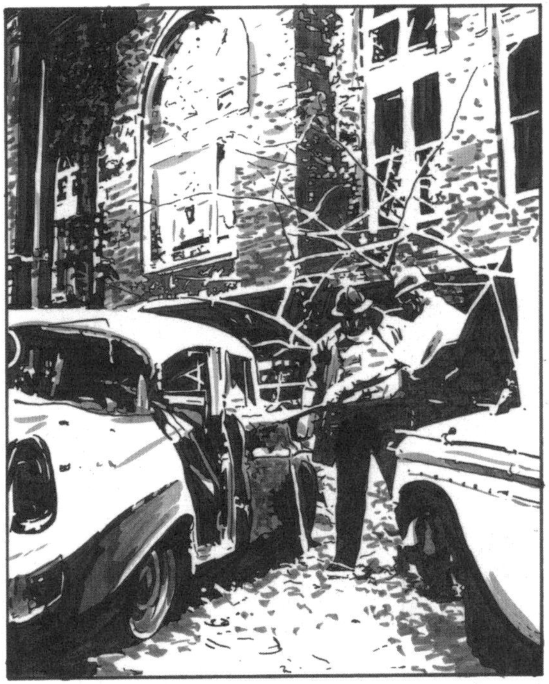

Curiously, though, an abandoned, burnt-out automobile was discovered some eight blocks from the apartment where The Specialist is believed to have lived.

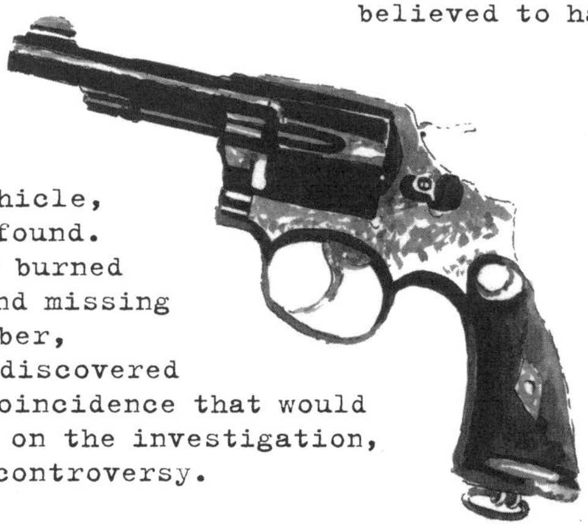

Inside that vehicle, a handgun was found. Although badly burned by the fire, and missing its serial number, investigators discovered a disturbing coincidence that would shed new light on the investigation, and even more controversy.

It seems that one of the investigators on the case discovered that Dizzy Walters
was a registered owner of the same model of handgun. When asked about the gun,
Dizzy Walters' attorney responded that the gun had been
missing for years-- presumably stolen.

The alleged theft was never reported.

The discovery of the gun would cause some to speculate that
The Specialist was, in fact, Dizzy Walters himself.

A photo was then discovered further supporting that possibility and fueling
the speculation. The photo, and the ensuing investigation, revealed that
Dizzy Walters served as a medic in England during the First World War.

Could Dizzy Walters, himself, have been the notorious "Specialist?"

OH, I DON'T DOUBT IT FOR A MINUTE!
IT'S ALL ABOUT THE MONEY!
WHATEVER IT TAKES TO TURN A PROFIT.
I HAVE NO PROBLEM BELIEVING IT AT ALL.

I... I DON'T KNOW....
HE WAS A.... A GOOD MAN.
I DON'T KNOW.

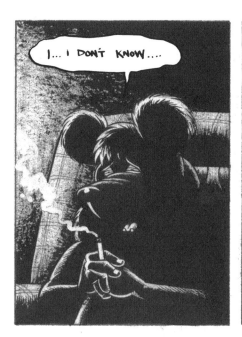

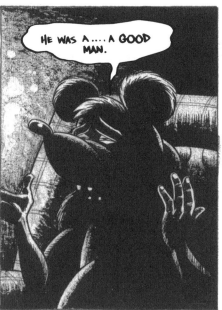

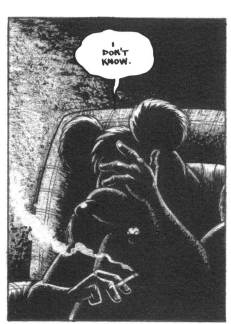

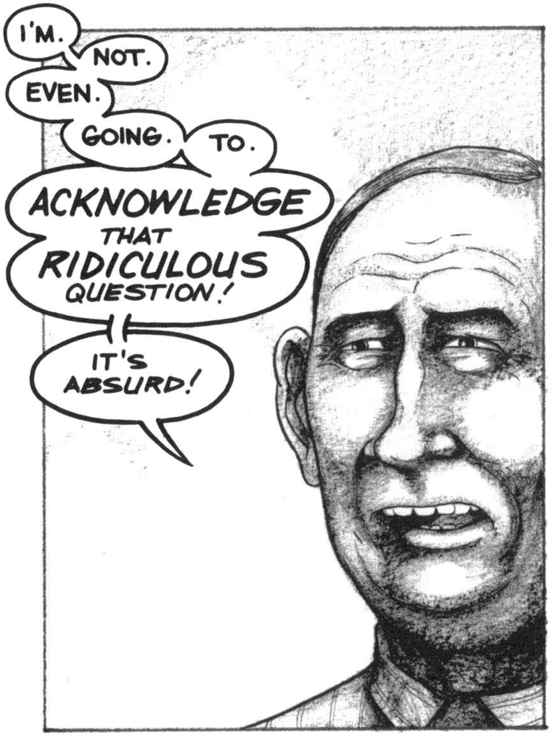
I'M.
NOT.
EVEN.
GOING.
TO.
ACKNOWLEDGE THAT RIDICULOUS QUESTION!
IT'S ABSURD!

Regardless of whom exactly The Specialist was, during the short period of time he allegedly performed his operations, more big Toon Stars emerged than in all the years before or since.

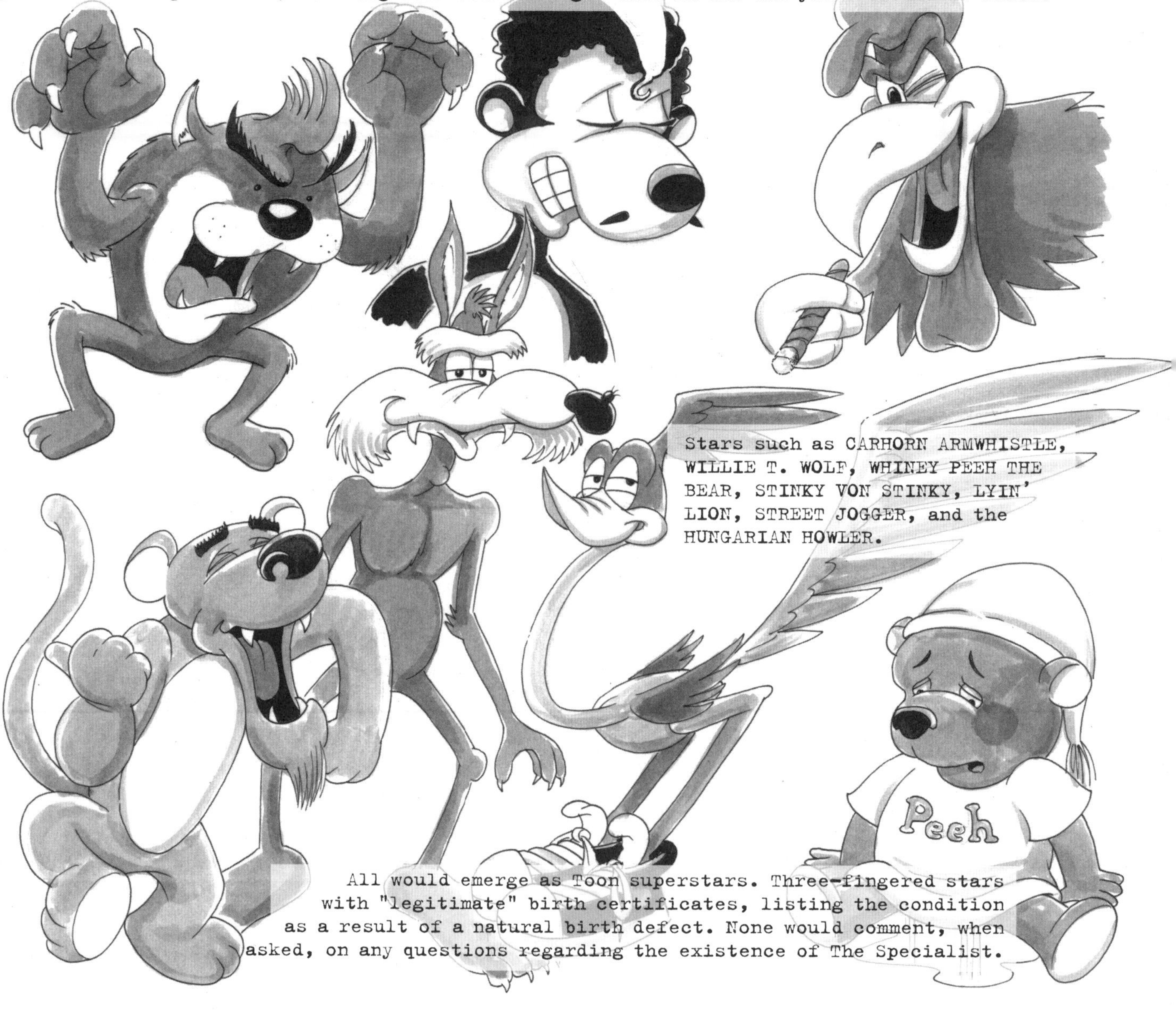
Peeh

Stars such as CARHORN ARMWHISTLE, WILLIE T. WOLF, WHINEY PEEH THE BEAR, STINKY VON STINKY, LYIN' LION, STREET JOGGER, and the HUNGARIAN HOWLER.

All would emerge as Toon superstars. Three-fingered stars with "legitimate" birth certificates, listing the condition as a result of a natural birth defect. None would comment, when asked, on any questions regarding the existence of The Specialist.

Yes, more and more stars were emerging,
and the cartoon industry was reaching new and uncharted heights.

But just as it was reaching its pinnacle,
something tragic would happen, and its timing would further the speculation
that Dizzy Walters and The Specialist were, indeed, one and the same.

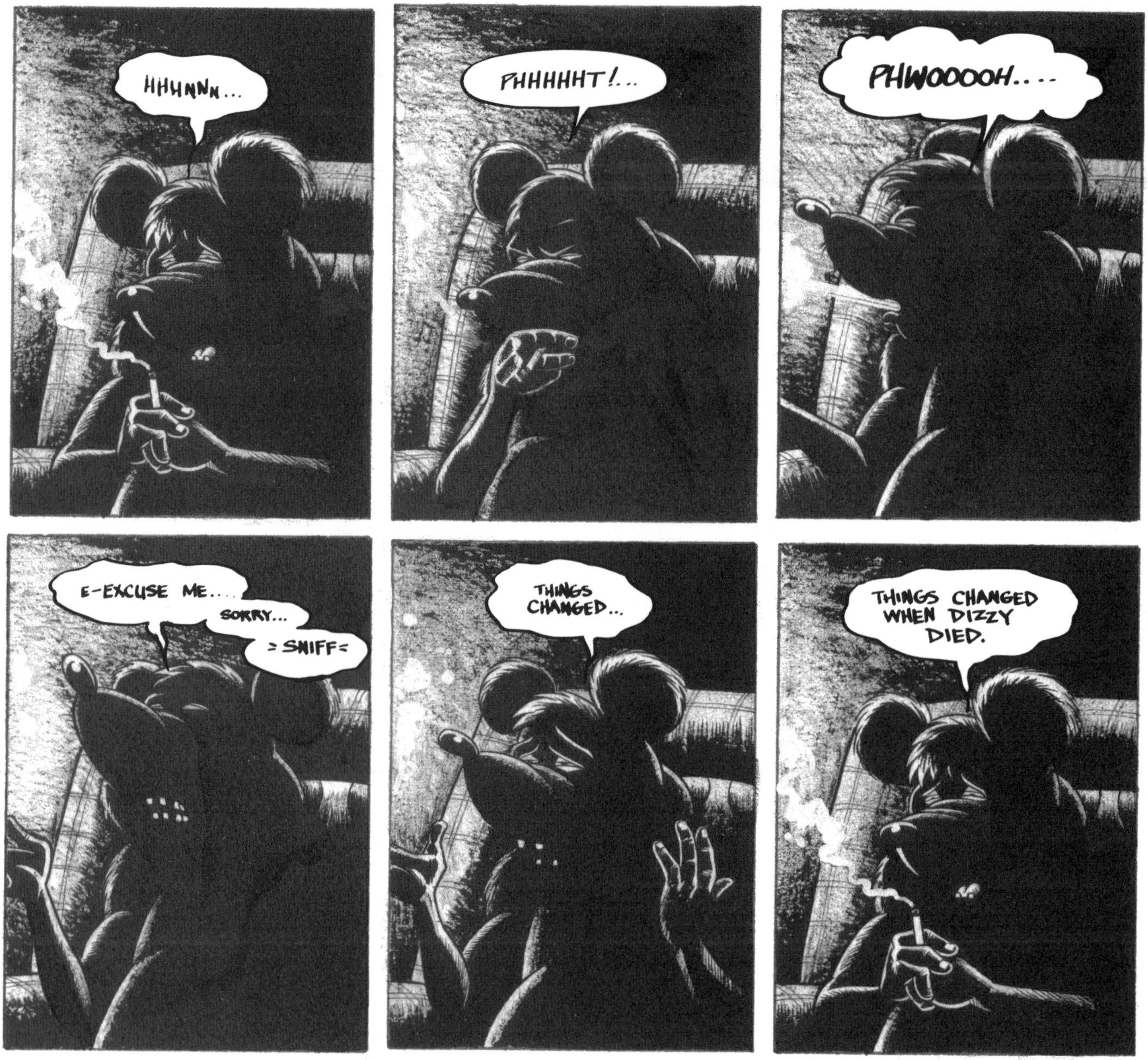
HHHNNN...
PHHHHHT!...
PHWOOOOH....
E-EXCUSE ME....
SORRY...
=SNIFF=
THINGS CHANGED...
THINGS CHANGED WHEN DIZZY DIED.

END OF AN ERA

By the late 1950s, the cartoon industry had seen its fair share of failure and success.

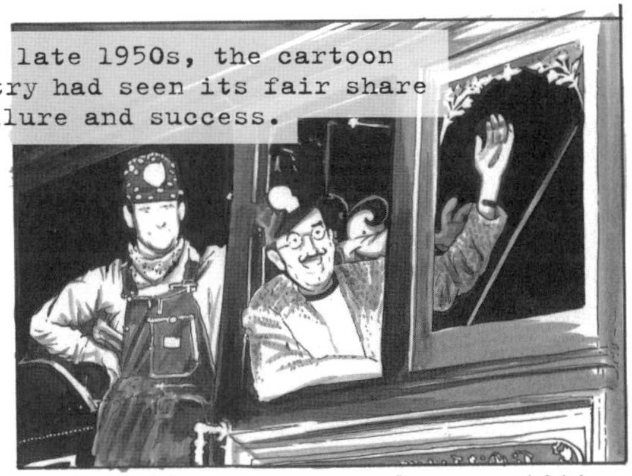

Failure, success, superstition, controversy, and bad habits.

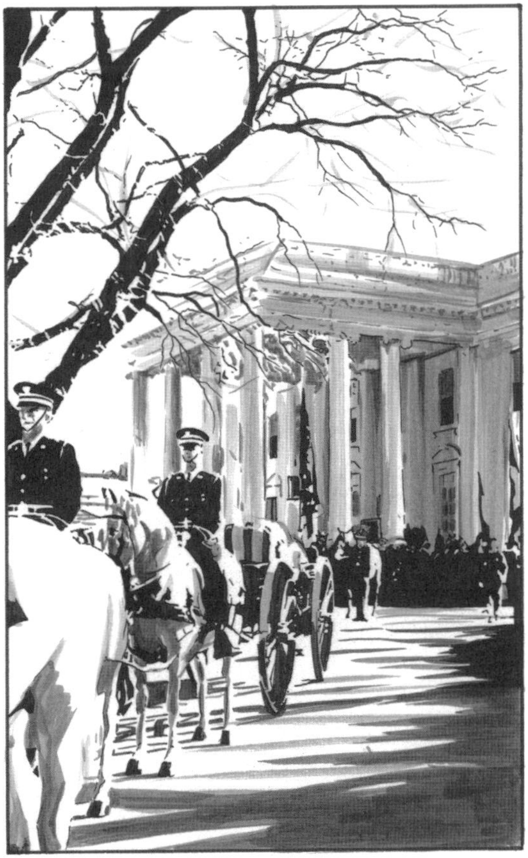

But as time goes on and superstitions fade, habits tend to die... people die, too.

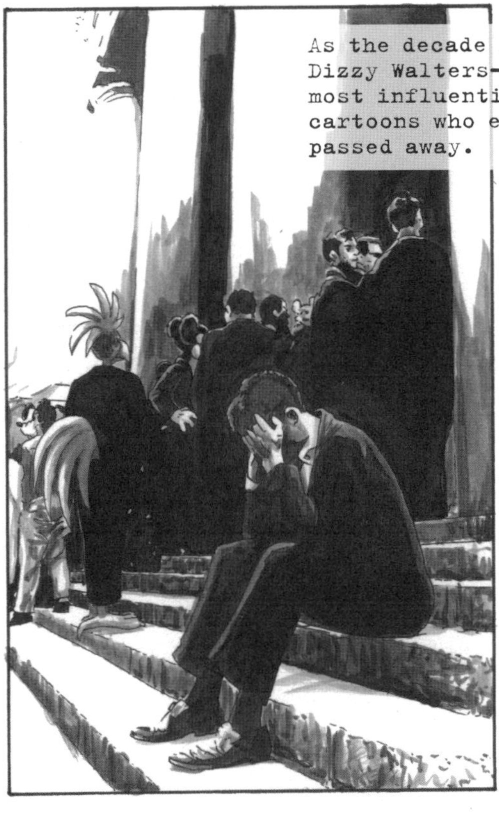

As the decade neared its end, Dizzy Walters-- the greatest, most influential producer of cartoons who ever lived, passed away.

And with him, many of the myths surrounding his and Rickey's uncanny success.

One myth, however, would live on.

The timing of Dizzy's death and the disappearance of The Specialist, coupled with the somewhat inflammatory evidence revealed thereafter, were just too strong of coincidences for some to ever dismiss.

The new executives now in charge at Dizzy Walters Studios worked quickly to dispel any negative publicity surrounding Dizzy's death. They announced that they would continue on with a project that Dizzy had begun working on at the time of his death.

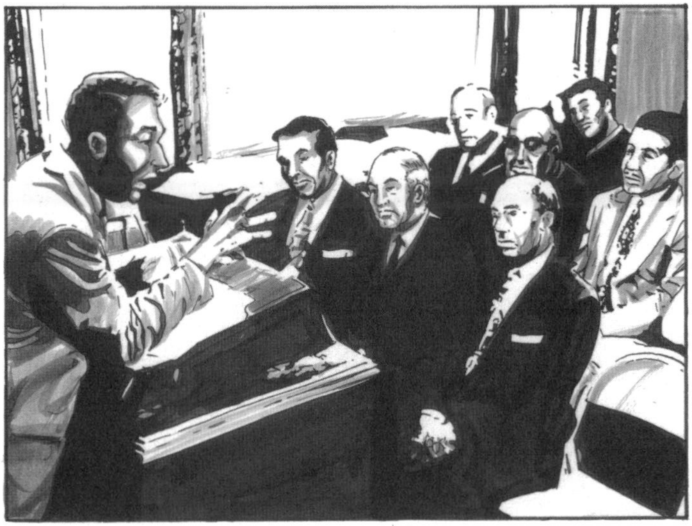

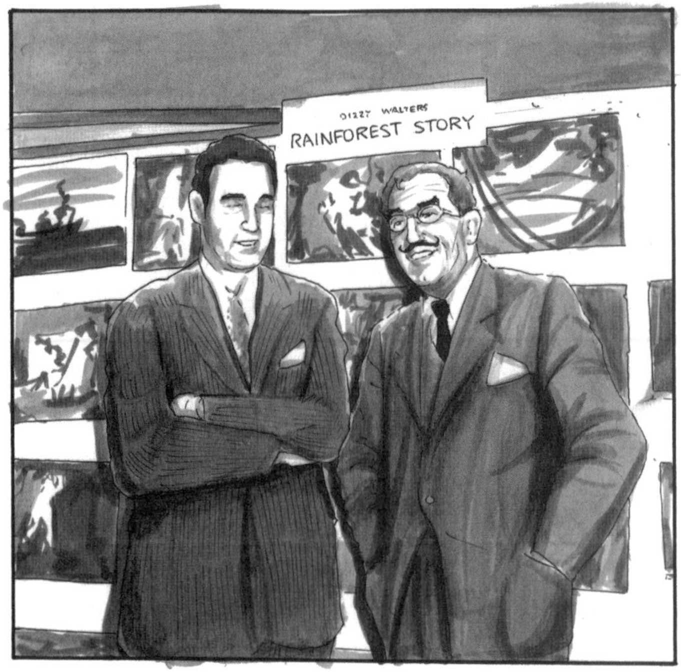
DIZZY WALTERS
RAINFOREST STORY

A project Dizzy was determined to produce that would prove, once and for all, Dizzy Walters Studios put no stock in the belief that only three-fingered Toons could succeed.

The project, "THE RAINFOREST STORY," would star a young Toon of Asian descent, named CHOW-MOW GLEE.

A four-fingered Toon.

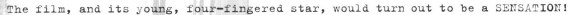

The film, and its young, four-fingered star, would turn out to be a SENSATION!

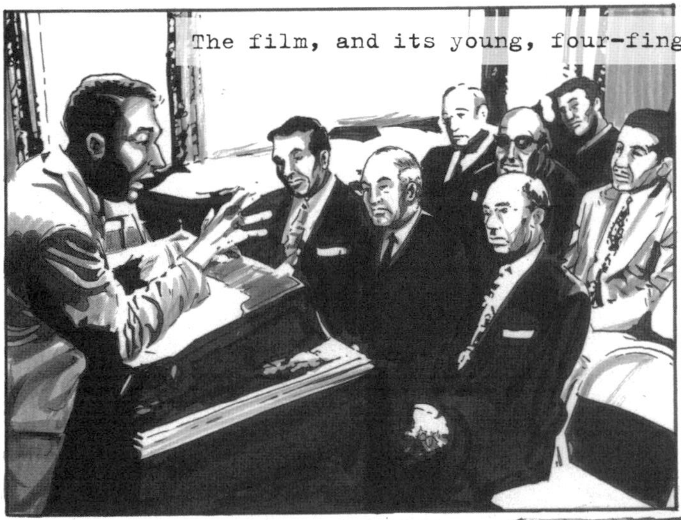

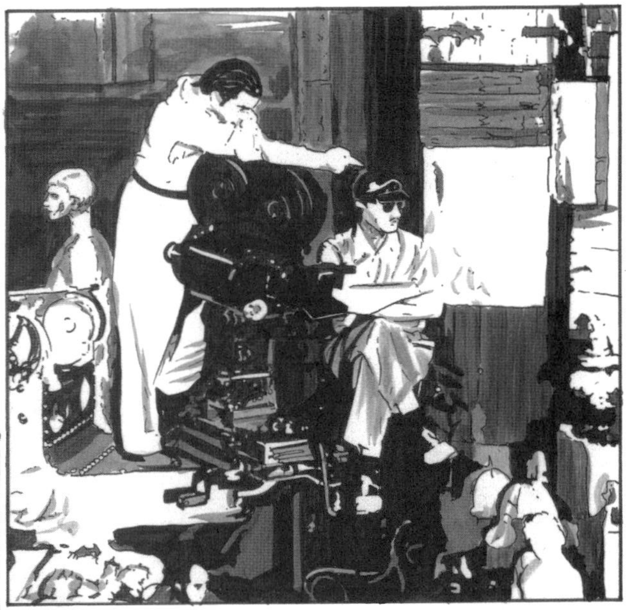

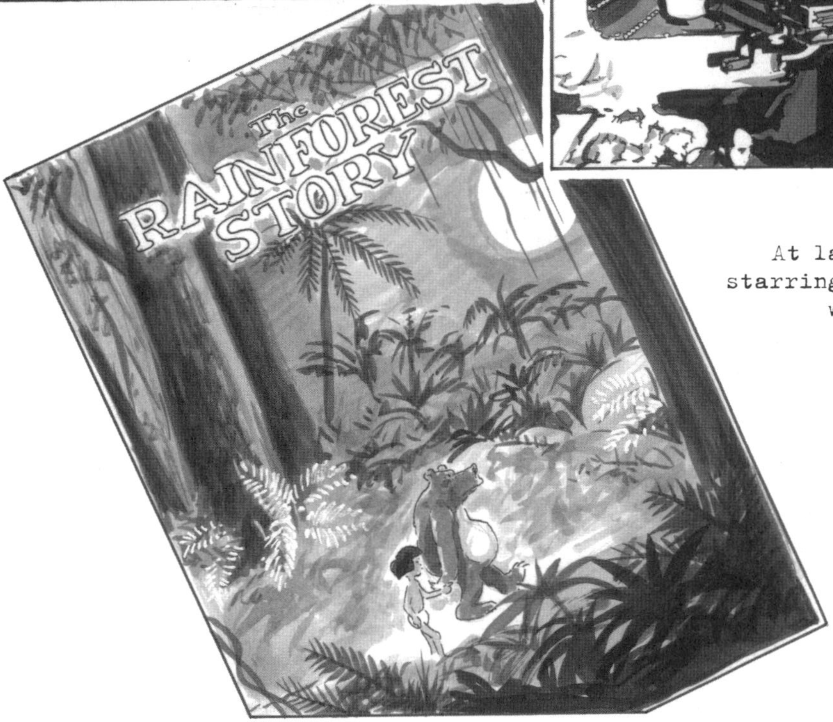
The RAINFOREST STORY

At last, a successful film
starring a four-fingered Toon
was made, thus proving
the old rumors and
superstitions wrong.

"RAINFOREST" AND CHOW MOW-G[] TOP BOX OFFICE!

FOUR-FINGERED 'TO[] GETS FOUR STARS!

Rumors of Dizzy's connection
to The Specialist were
quickly forgotten.

"RAINFORES[] LIVES ON! AND C[] TOP BOX O[]

DIZZY WALTERS LEGACY LIVES ON!

SIAN 'TOON GETS TWO THUMBS U[] AND EIGHT FINGERS!

CHOW MOW-GLEE AN INTERNATIONAL SENSATION!

His legacy was,
once again, intact.

"RAINFOREST STORY" A SMASH!

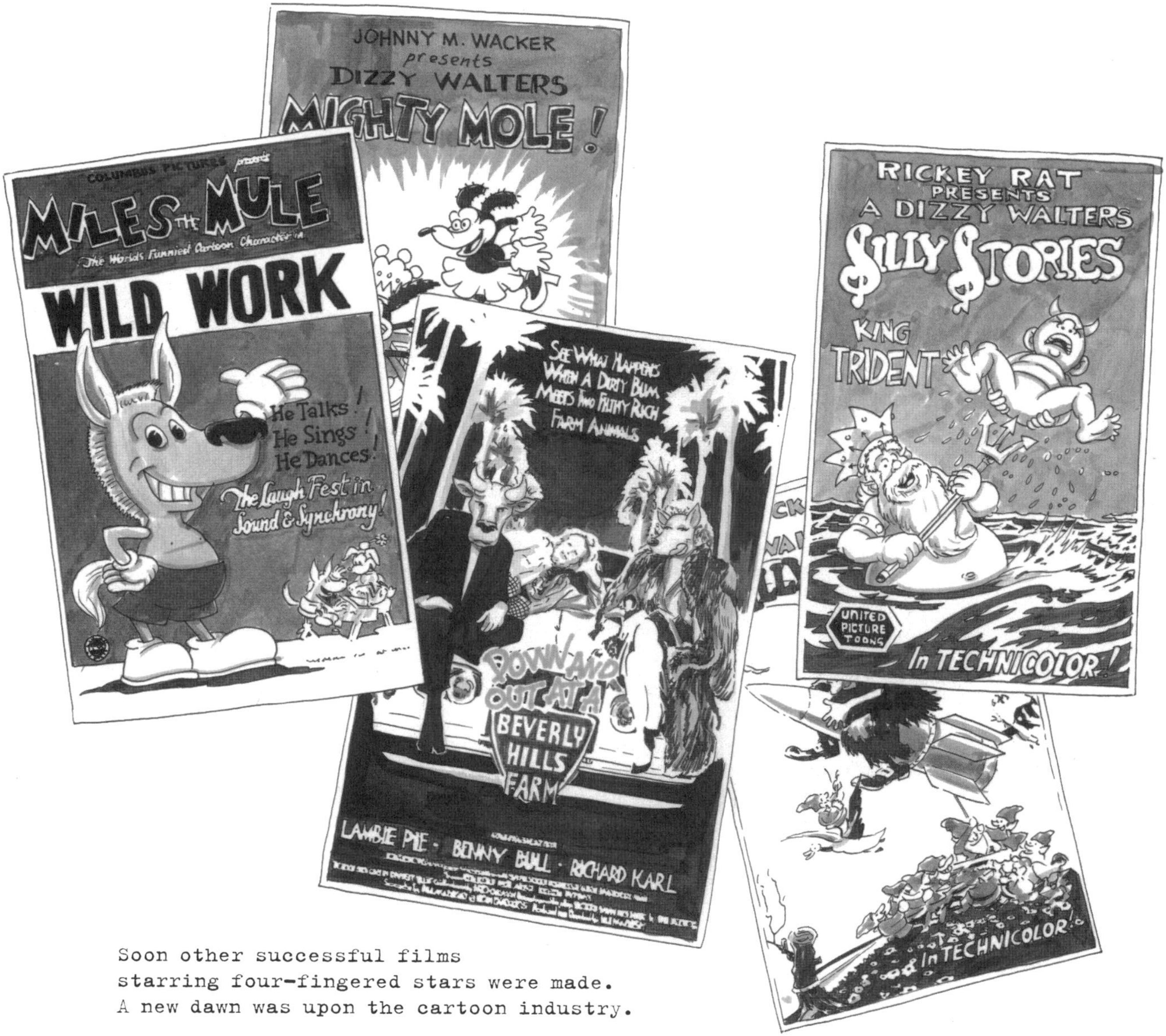
JOHNNY M. WACKER
presents
DIZZY WALTERS
MIGHTY MOLE!
COLUMBUS PICTURES presents
MILES THE MULE
The World's Funniest Cartoon Character in
WILD WORK
He Talks!
He Sings!
He Dances!
The Laugh Fest in Sound & Synchrony!
SEE WHAT HAPPENS WHEN A DIRTY BUM MEETS TWO FILTHY RICH FARM ANIMALS
DOWN AND OUT AT A BEVERLY HILLS FARM
LAMBIE PIE · BENNY BULL · RICHARD KARL
RICKEY RAT
PRESENTS
A DIZZY WALTERS
SILLY STORIES
KING TRIDENT
UNITED PICTURE TOONS
In TECHNICOLOR!
In TECHNICOLOR!

Soon other successful films
starring four-fingered stars were made.
A new dawn was upon the cartoon industry.

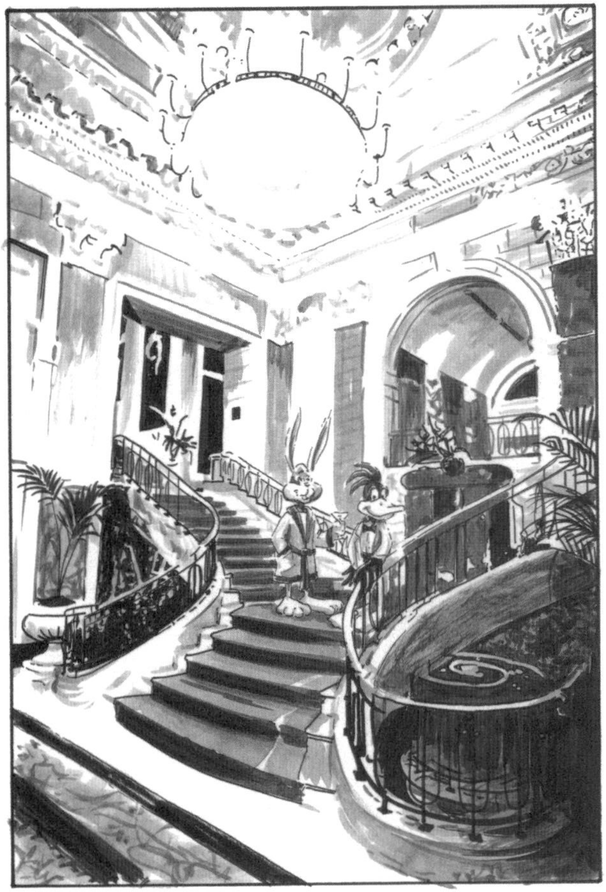

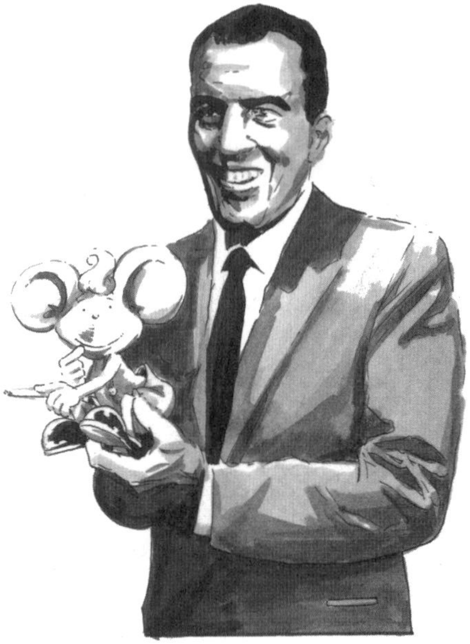

Three and four-fingered stars
alike were thriving.

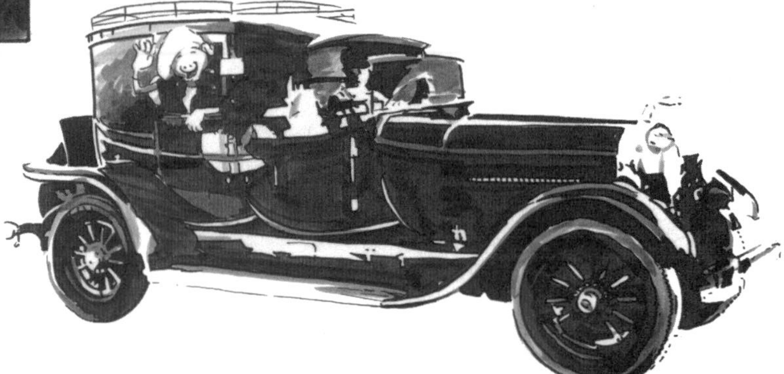

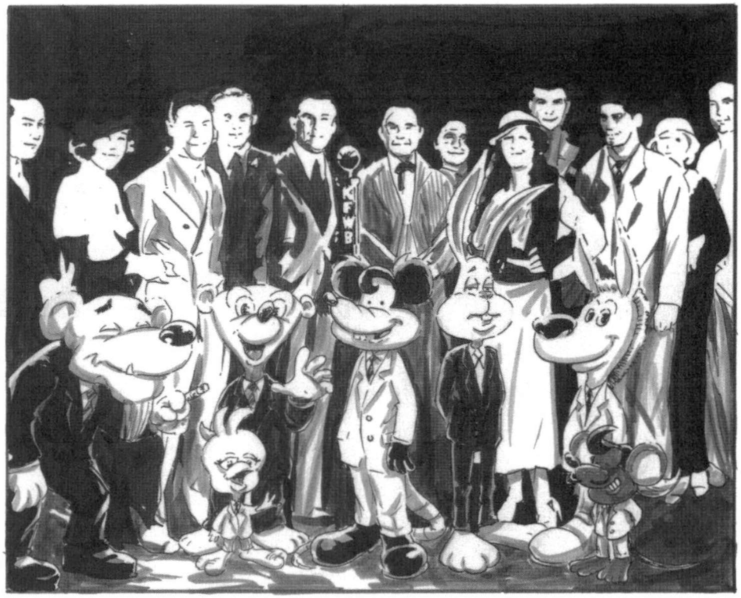
KFWB

Everyone was happy.

YEAH.... EVERYONE WAS HAPPY.
FOR AWHILE AT LEAST.

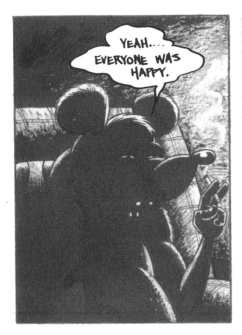

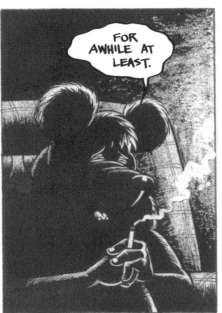

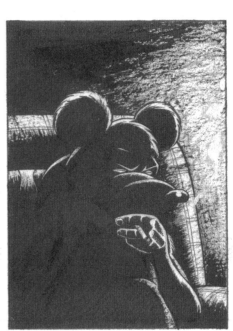

Still, only a short while
after the release of
"The Rainforest Story",
a new rumor surfaced,
claiming that Chow-Mow Glee
did, IN FACT, have only
three fingers, and that
Dizzy Walters Studios had
fourth fingers added to his
hands, frame by frame, during
post-production of the film.

Unfortunately, the rumors can be neither confirmed, nor denied,
since the young actor has never been seen since the making of the
movie finished, and the original
print of the film was destroyed
in a warehouse fire.

Several years after Chow-Mow Glee's disappearance from the public eye, investigators Robert Gilbertson and Floyd Patton captured this footage of, allegedly, an older Chow-Mow Glee running from their cameras.

It is difficult to be certain, but magnified views seem to show what appear to be only THREE FINGERS on the running figure's right hand.

The now-famous GILBERTSON-PATTON FILM would once again cast doubt and confusion amongst the Toon community.

And that is why, to this day, you will still see the occasional new Toon Star with only THREE FINGERS on his hand.

ALL THIS... ALL BECAUSE OF ME...
WHY?! WHY DO THESE FOOLS STILL BUY INTO THAT 'RITUAL' CRAP?!
I... I GUESS SOME HABITS JUST DIE HARDER THAN OTHERS.

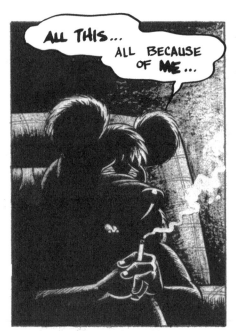

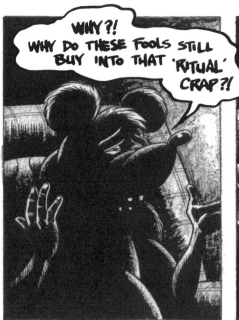

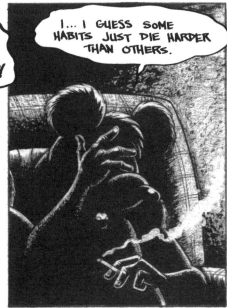

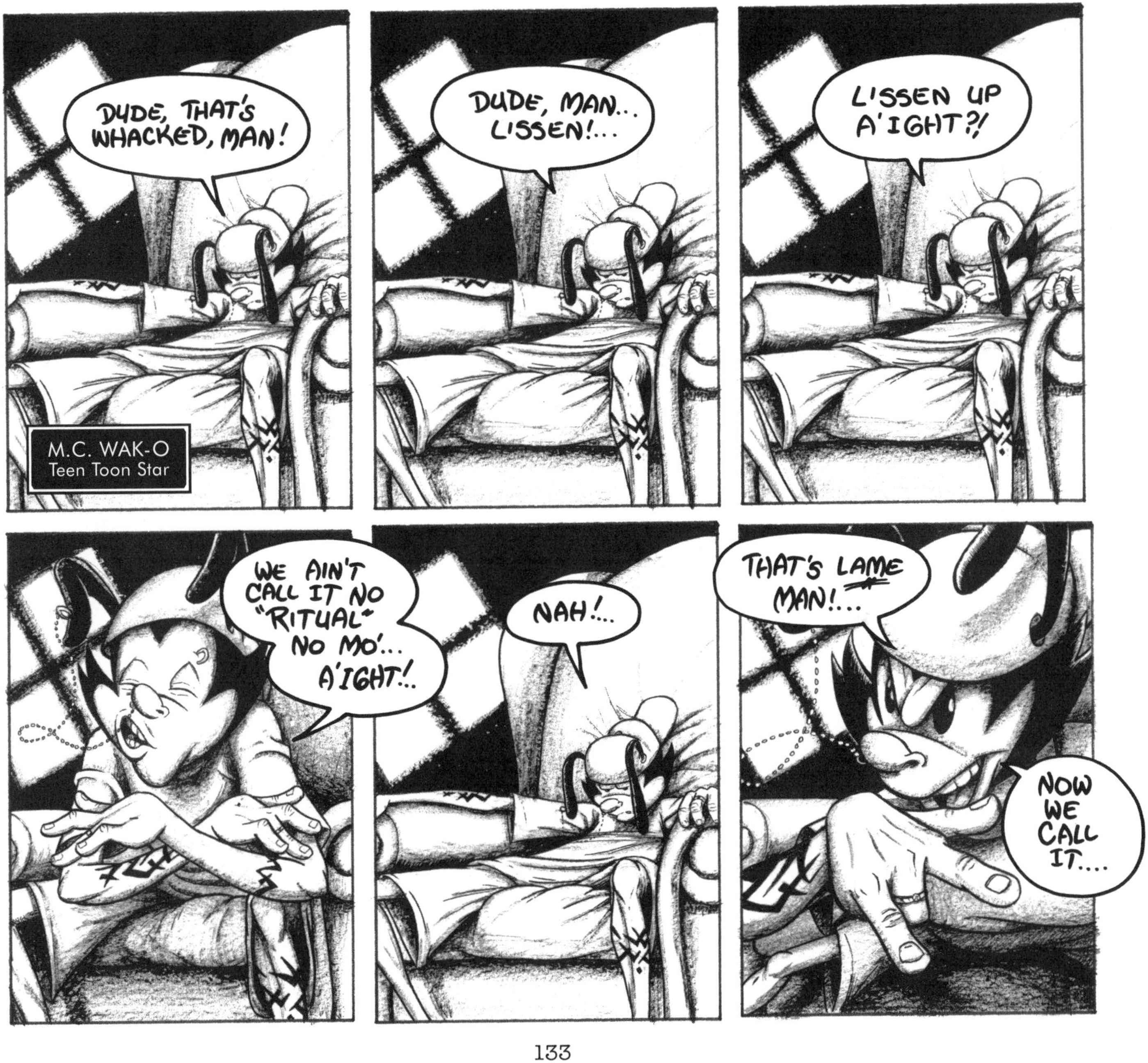
DUDE, THAT'S WHACKED, MAN!
M.C. WAK-O
Teen Toon Star
DUDE, MAN... LISSEN!...
LISSEN UP A'IGHT?!
WE AIN'T CALL IT NO "RITUAL" NO MO'... A'IGHT!..
NAH!...
THAT'S LAME MAN!...
NOW WE CALL IT....

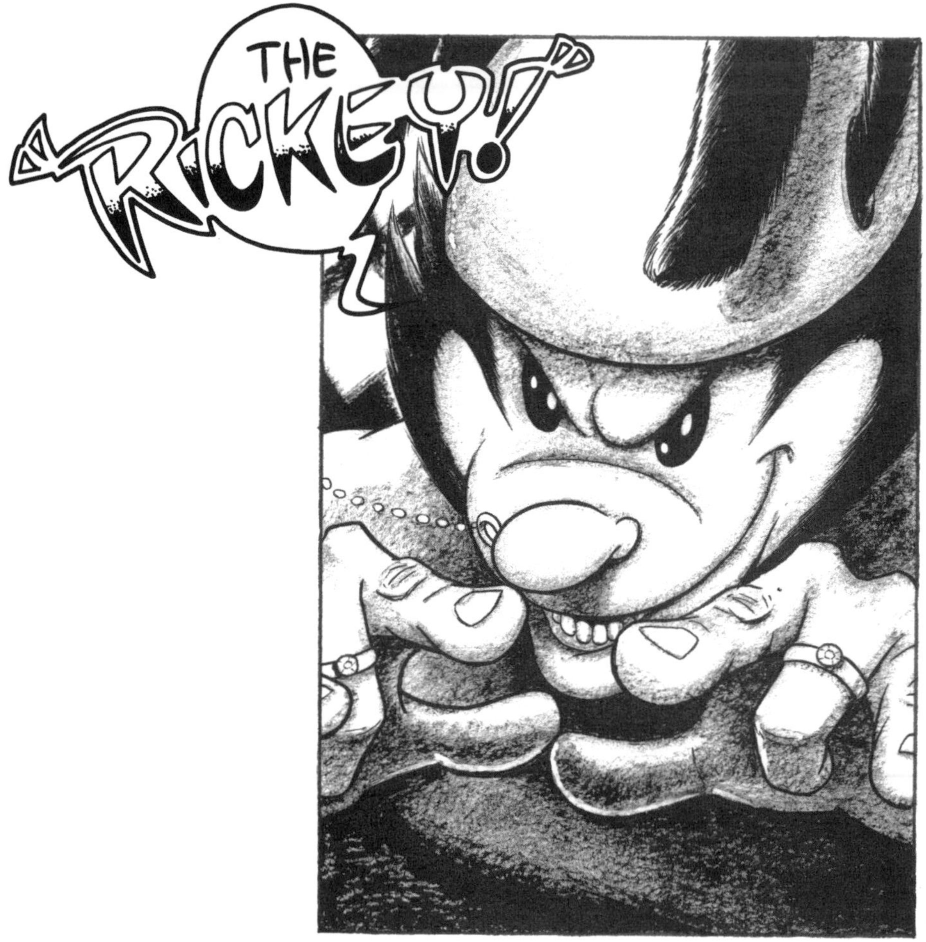
THE
RICKEY!

THE END

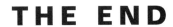

This book is dedicated to my girls, Sandy and Stella.
The sun and stars in my life.

I would like to give my most heartfelt thanks to the following people: First and foremost my wife, and best friend, Sandy. Without her none of this would be possible. Chris and Brett for so strongly believing in this project. My good buddies Jason Asala and C.J. Bettin who helped me out with all the computer crap. Their help was invaluable and I am greatly in their debt. To Steve Leaf from Diamond Comics for his amazing support of this project. To Alan David Doane from COMIC BOOK GALAXY for his encouraging review and help with spotting all my typos. To Tony Isabella for his very kind advance review of this book in the COMIC BUYER'S GUIDE. To all of those who have critically supported me over the years on THE 3 GEEKS and GEEKSVILLE. To all of my readers who have been incredibly devoted. To all the wonderful retailers who continue to take chances on smaller publishers, especially my man Chuck Rozanski, who continues to show the most overwhelmingly generous support. To Steve Borock, Gary Sassaman, The Fallcon Crew, Jonah Weiland, Batton Lash, Jackie Estrada, Jeff Smith and John Kovalic... just a few who have shown me support over the years. To Diamond, for all of the support in the past and whose help I greatly appreciate. To my mom and dad... they're always there when we need them. To our families... hey, they're our families!

And finally, to my little girl, Stella. My newest inspiration in this world.

Author/Artist, Rich Koslowski, shown here holding a giant pumpkin his wife, Sandy, found growing in the backyard.

"It was the weirdest thing," said Koslowski, "The year before I threw our old, rotted Halloween pumpkins back behind the shed... y'know... and then, the next summer, Sandy comes in the house and tells me, 'You gotta come see this!' I was totally freaked!"

Koslowski has worked for the past 20 years in the Comic Book, Animation and Children's Book industries. He is best known for his critically acclaimed work with Top Shelf Productions on THREE FINGERS and THE KING.

He is also well known for his fan-favorite comic book, THE 3 GEEKS (GEEKSVILLE) which was nominated for three Eisner Awards.

In 2003, THREE FINGERS was nominated for the Ignatz, Harvey and Ursa Major awards for "Outstanding Graphic Novel," winning the coveted Ignatz. In 2008, THREE FINGERS was included in the "500 Essential Graphic Novels: The Ultimate Guide" by Harper Collins/ Collins Design.

In 2010, his latest graphic novel, BB WOLF AND THE 3 LPs, written by his friend, J.D. Arnold, will be released by Top Shelf.

After 41 years of brutal winters, Rich and Sandy finally said enough to Wisconsin and packed up and moved to Aptos, CA. They brought Stella, too!

They no longer hate the weather.

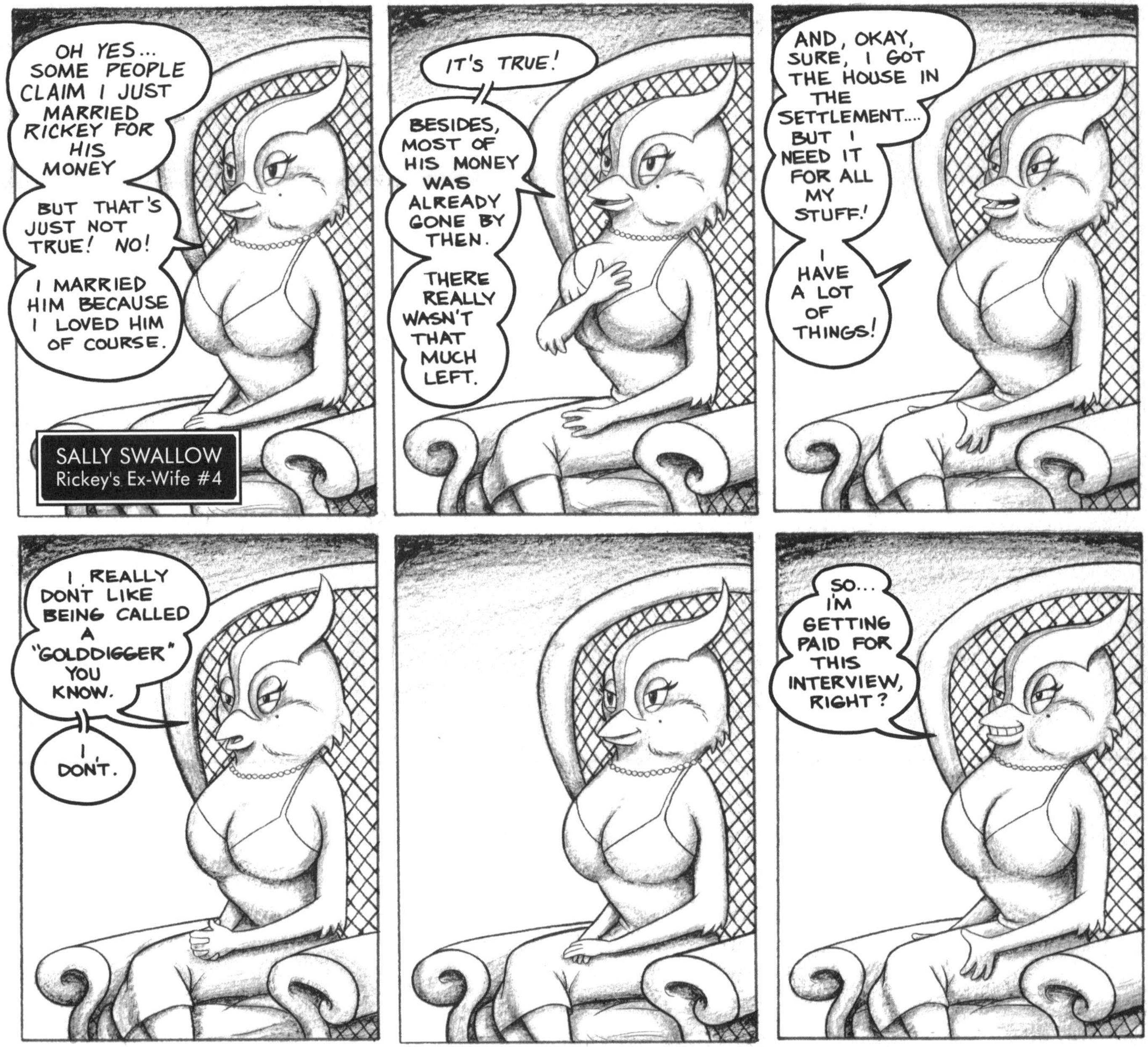
OH YES... SOME PEOPLE CLAIM I JUST MARRIED RICKEY FOR HIS MONEY
BUT THAT'S JUST NOT TRUE! NO!
I MARRIED HIM BECAUSE I LOVED HIM OF COURSE.
SALLY SWALLOW
Rickey's Ex-Wife #4
IT'S TRUE!
BESIDES, MOST OF HIS MONEY WAS ALREADY GONE BY THEN.
THERE REALLY WASN'T THAT MUCH LEFT.
AND, OKAY, SURE, I GOT THE HOUSE IN THE SETTLEMENT.... BUT I NEED IT FOR ALL MY STUFF!
I HAVE A LOT OF THINGS!
I REALLY DON'T LIKE BEING CALLED A "GOLDDIGGER" YOU KNOW.
I DON'T.
SO... I'M GETTING PAID FOR THIS INTERVIEW, RIGHT?